Unclaimed Property

Unclaimed Property

A Reporting Process and Audit Survival Guide

TRACEY L. REID

WILEY

John Wiley & Sons, Inc.

Library of Congress Cataloging-in-Publication Data

Reid, Tracey L.
    Unclaimed property : a reporting process and audit survival guide / Tracey L. Reid.
       p. cm.
    Includes index.
    ISBN 978-0-470-27824-6 (cloth)
    1. Abandonment of property—United States.   2. Escheat—United States.   3. Abandonment of property—United States—Auditing.   I. Title.
    KF562.R45 2008
    346.7304'7—dc22

                                                                    2008017692

Printed in the United States of America
10 9 8 7 6 5 4 3 2 1

To my husband Anthony for all his love, support, and the creative ways that he distracted our kids; and to the rest of my family for their encouragement, faith, and free babysitting services:
Thank you

Contents

Preface

For many of my clients, the first time they heard of "unclaimed property" was when they were notified that their company had been chosen for an unclaimed property audit and needed to dig out ten years of old financial records to present to an auditor for review. Unclaimed property law enforcement has recently become the darling of politicians across the country who are looking for ways to increase their states' revenues without instituting new taxes that alienate their voters. While unclaimed property laws have been on the books in all states for many years, only in the past decade have those laws really been enforced against businesses outside the banking industry. To speed up the collection of unclaimed property, state laws are changing rapidly every year. While it can be almost impossible to understand the intricacies of all of the different state laws, it IS possible to bring your company into compliance with the escheat laws you are subject to.

I have been teaching unclaimed property seminars across the country for the last several years, and the attendees always ask the same question: "Where can I get a book on unclaimed property to help me get my company into shape?" Unfortunately, in the past, I've never had a good answer for them. There are several very formidable and well-researched legal treatises available on the subject of unclaimed property law, but there has been no practical guide geared toward the over-extended businessperson who just wants to make sure his or her company is compliant—*until now.*

This book is not intended to make you an expert on unclaimed property law. It is intended to help you understand the nature of the escheat laws and how they affect your company's bottom line. I will help you calculate your company's actual unclaimed property exposure; come up with a plan to get into compliance, and guide you through a planning process that will keep your company compliant into the future. My goal is to prepare you to handle any unclaimed property enquiry that will come across your desk, whether it is a former employee looking for a "lost" paycheck, your internal auditor questioning how you handle outstanding checks, or a state administrator requesting information on your company's unreported unclaimed property. I will break the process down into manageable steps that you can handle either on your own or with the help of a professional in the field. Unclaimed property compliance can become just another process in your company, rather than a ticking time bomb buried in your financials, ready to detonate upon audit.

This book is not just for escheat beginners. If you are already reporting unclaimed property and have systems in place, this book can help you conduct your own checkup to find areas that may need improvement. I will also address how to deal with unclaimed property audits, something that can and will happen to *every* business, whether you have never reported or have been in compliance with the escheat laws since the day your business opened its doors. I will provide you with state contact information and a few charts that my clients have found helpful in the past. This book includes sample due diligence letters and a sample policy and procedures manual to get you started in your own departments. As changes occur, I will post updated charts on my Web site for your reference. I hope that this manual will be a tool you reference over and over again when you have questions about unclaimed property.

If you have any further questions, feel free to contact me at treid@ reidunclaimed.com or to post a question in our chat room at www .reidunclaimed.com.

CHAPTER 1

Four Myths of
Unclaimed Property

Myth 1: "We Don't Have Unclaimed Property."

All companies have unclaimed property. If your company writes checks; issues gift certificates or gift cards; writes employee expense reimbursement checks; or issues vendor credits; you have unclaimed property. If you write checks, you have unclaimed property until every single one is cashed. If you issue credits in your accounting system, you have unclaimed property until every credit is used. Since *unclaimed property* is generally defined as *tangible or intangible property that has gone unclaimed by its rightful owner,* every check, vendor credit, gift certificate, and payroll electronic transfer is unclaimed property until it is cashed, offset, redeemed, or accepted into a valid account. *Every business has unclaimed property.* This book will help you answer the important question: *"Is my outstanding unclaimed property reportable to any state unclaimed property office?"*

Myth 2: "Unclaimed Property Compliance is Voluntary."

Unclaimed property compliance is *mandatory* in all 50 states, the District of Columbia, Puerto Rico, the U.S. Virgin Islands, and Guam. Several other countries also have unclaimed property laws (see Chapter 9, Foreign Unclaimed Property Laws). Compliance does not just mean you are reporting the unclaimed property that you know you have. Compliance, in some states, means that you are filing a report telling the states that you have *no* unclaimed property that is reportable that year. Several states, such as Ohio, require that every business that is registered to do business in that state file an unclaimed property report *every year,* even if they have no property to turn over for that period. This is called a *negative report* or a *zero report.* Not every type of business is required to report unclaimed property in all of the U.S. states and territories, but all of these governing bodies are collecting unclaimed property from *some* businesses. For example, the escheat laws in Guam only govern dormant bank accounts, but every bank that does business in Guam or has customers with a last known address of record in Guam could be subject to reporting unclaimed property to that territory. I will help you pinpoint all of the areas where your company is required to file unclaimed property reports in this book.

MYTH 3: "IF I DON'T HAVE RECORDS, THE AUDITOR CAN'T DETERMINE ANY UNCLAIMED PROPERTY LIABILITY FOR MY COMPANY."

In the absence of records, auditors are permitted to use estimation techniques to determine a holder's unclaimed property liability. Many of my clients have historically followed the federal government's seven-year tax record retention policy for all of their financial records. For unclaimed property purposes, this gets them into a heap of trouble. Unclaimed Property is not a tax. It is a *property law.* As such, it is generally *not* subject to any statute of limitations. Only a few states provide for any statute of limitations, and even then the statute only applies if the holder properly reported to the correct government agency in a timely manner. The typical unclaimed property audit covers a period of ten to fifteen years, which is much longer than the federal government's tax record retention period. If a holder, like most businesses, does not have financial records for the entire audit period, auditors use the most current records to project what the old records *might* have looked like. If your company has had recent periods of growth, but was smaller 15 years ago, today's records are going to produce a much inflated picture of what your historic unclaimed property reporting liability actually was. There are several ways to estimate your unclaimed property in the absence of actual records, and you can negotiate with auditors to use the projection method most beneficial to your company's situation. We will discuss how to handle your records (or lack of them) later in Chapter 4.

MYTH 4: "I AM ONLY LIABLE FOR REPORTING UNCLAIMED PROPERTY TO STATES WHERE I CONDUCT BUSINESS (I.E., HAVE NEXUS)."

Unclaimed property is *not a tax!* There is no nexus requirement for your company to be subject to unclaimed property reporting. The U.S. Supreme Court has laid out the reporting pecking order for unclaimed property, and it has absolutely nothing to do with where your company is doing business. If you have an address in your records, then the last known address of the property's owner determines where it must be reported. Where your company is incorporated plays a part, but only if you do not have addresses for the true owner of the escheatable property. As companies do not always do business in the states where they are incorporated (i.e., Delaware), nexus can have absolutely NOTHING to do with your unclaimed property reporting obligations. We will address how you can get a handle on your unclaimed property reporting obligations in Chapter 6.

Why all the fuss about unclaimed property? As of 2005, a total of $20 billion worth of unclaimed property was in state coffers, and only about 20% of that money is ever returned to the true owners. This means that the states get both the benefit of interest earned on the assets being held and, in some cases, the actual escheated property after a period of years. Unclaimed property is the fastest growing source of state revenue— and it's increasing 20% per year!

The country's state unclaimed property administrators estimate that only 10% to 20% of U.S. businesses currently comply with escheat laws. That leaves 80% to 90% either unaware of their reporting obligations or too overwhelmed by the process of coming into compliance to know where to begin. First-time audits of previously noncompliant companies typically reach back a minimum of 10 years, but some reach back as far as 20 years. In most states, there is no statute of limitations for unclaimed property compliance. Filing a negative or zero report does NOT start any statute of limitations running to limit your company's exposure. You may think, for example, that you are safe from audits because you are compliant with the unclaimed property laws in your incorporation state, but do not count on it! States are joining forces and sending audit teams all over the country with the authority to audit on behalf of multiple states. Many states are signing contracts with third-party audit firms that do not get paid their 10% to 15% unless they find unclaimed property owing to any of the 31 states with which they have agreements. And your audit threat is not limited to being fingered by a state auditor. States have passed "whistle-blower" laws to encourage individuals with knowledge of a company's noncompliance to come forward and share the wealth. A whistle-blower typically gets 10% of what the state collects in an unclaimed property audit as a reward. If you have any disgruntled ex-employees, or current employees who want to retire early on your dime, you need to get into unclaimed property compliance.

Keeping track of the unclaimed property compliance is a full-time job for most businesses. There is currently no uniform set of laws that apply to all states; each state, district, or territory has its own laws, which amounts to 54 different jurisdictions, including all 50 states, the District of Columbia, Guam, Puerto Rico, and the U.S. Virgin Islands! Do you have time to keep track of the legislative changes every year? Do you have the resources to assign this task to someone in your organization?

When state revenues go down, unclaimed property audit efforts go up. Every company registered to do business will eventually be contacted for an unclaimed property audit, but early preparation can make all the difference in what that audit ultimately costs. While many businesses make decisions for their company's future based on tax laws, very few, if any, plan their growth around unclaimed property laws—nor should they. This book is meant to help businesspeople understand what unclaimed property is, how the escheat laws apply to their particular circumstances, and how they can bring their enterprises into compliance with the least amount of manpower and cash outlay possible. You *can* comply with unclaimed property laws without going either crazy or bankrupt, and I will show you how.

CHAPTER 2

What Is Unclaimed Property?

Unclaimed property laws might be new to you, but they have been around for millennia. The ancient Romans had officers whose duty was to collect the property, on behalf of the emperor, of persons who died without heirs or legatees. The English, during the reign of William the Conqueror, instituted laws that claimed property, both real and personal, on behalf of the Crown when someone died without heirs or committed certain types of crimes. Escheat was specifically mentioned in England's Magna Carta, written in 1215. When our forefathers came to the colonies, they brought their traditional law, English common law, with them.

Originating from an old French term meaning change or accident, *escheat* is the means by which land returned to the tenant's lord or the Crown when some event interrupted the normal course of descent, such as when someone died without leaving an heir.[1] In the early common-law era, the escheat laws only dealt with real property. *Bona vacantia,* meaning vacant or ownerless goods, was the way that the Crown claimed abandoned personal property against everyone but the rightful owner. In the United States, *the states,* not the federal government, are the benefactors of the escheat and *bona vacantia* laws.

Over the years, the states have worked together and attempted to make one universal set of unclaimed property laws that could be applied across the country to simplify unclaimed property reporting and collection. The first attempt by the National Conference of Commissioners on Uniform State Laws (NCCUSL) produced the Uniform Disposition of Unclaimed Property Act of 1954. This Act has been adopted, either in whole or in part, by 12 states. The states that still follow this Act are Arizona, California, Florida, Idaho, Illinois, Montana, New Mexico, Oregon, Utah, Virginia, Washington, and West Virginia.[2] Its primary characteristics are that it is custodial in nature, making the states the custodians of unclaimed property on behalf of the true owners; that it is comprehensive, in that it attempted to encompass all forms of intangible property; it was intended to be a consumer protection law; and it created revenue enhancement for the states, since they were allowed to benefit from interest earned from investing unclaimed funds in their care. This Act required due diligence efforts to be made by both the holders of the property and then by the state and obligated the states to keep records of the unclaimed property in their care forever. It also relieved the holders of liability toward the true owners once the property was reported and remitted to the states.

The Revised Uniform Disposition of Unclaimed Property Act of 1966 (NCCUSL) basically reiterated the 1954 Act, but added traveler's checks and money orders to the list of property covered by the unclaimed property laws. This 1966 Act was adopted by Illinois, Nebraska, and Pennsylvania and was also adopted in part, with modifications from the 1981 Act, by Mississippi and Missouri.[3]

The Uniform Unclaimed Property Act of 1981 (NCCUSL), adopted by another 26 states, the District of Columbia and the U.S. Virgin Islands, basically codified the Supreme Court's jurisdictional reporting requirements laid out in *Texas v. New Jersey*.[4] That case laid out the priority rules for reporting unclaimed property that we will discuss in Chapter 3. The states operating under this version of Uniform Unclaimed Property Act are Alaska, Colorado, Florida, Georgia, Hawaii, Idaho, Iowa, Maryland, Michigan, Minnesota, Nevada, New Hampshire, New Jersey, North Dakota, Tennessee, Utah, Vermont, Virginia, Washington, Wisconsin, and Wyoming.[5]

Still another Uniform Unclaimed Property Act was issued in 1995. The 1995 Act clarified some points raised by case law regarding stock certificates and provided further guidance to help businesses understand what the group felt: that the definition of a "holder" should focus on the obligation to pay an owner under state law, no matter whether the obligated party was the original debtor or not. This Act also allowed for civil penalties against noncompliant holders. This version of the Act has been accepted in ten states: Alabama, Arizona, Indiana, Kansas, Louisiana, Maine, Montana, New Mexico, North Carolina, and West Virginia.[6]

There are still a handful of states, including Delaware, Kentucky, Massachusetts, New York, Ohio, and Texas, which have not adopted ANY form of these Uniform Acts.[7] So much for "uniformity!"

Why is this history lesson important, you might ask? For two reasons. First, you need to understand that there is *no uniform set of unclaimed property laws*. The laws in each state and territory are different, and you need to understand the differences to keep your company in compliance. The most important state for you to be concerned with is your company's state of incorporation, which is the state *most* likely to audit you and is also the state that will probably collect the most unclaimed property from you. Second, you need to accept that, as uncomfortable as an unclaimed property audit may make your company, the law in the United States gives states the right to conduct them. Many different businesses and individuals have challenged the states' right to take this property in the past, but the courts have always sided with the states. Do not waste your company's resources trying to keep the state auditors out. The courts have ruled that escheat is a valid exercise of the state's power to regulate the succession to property, and the states have expanded the scope of the original escheat laws regarding realty to include the regulation of personal property in situations where the owner cannot be located. You cannot stop the auditors from coming, but you *can* mitigate the financial damage they leave in their wake by understanding your company's unclaimed property compliance status before they arrive.

Purpose of the Unclaimed Property Laws

The original purpose of abandoned property laws was to protect the interests of the true owners of unclaimed property until they could take control of it themselves. The states purport to be protecting the rights of individuals who have misplaced their valuable property, keeping that property safe instead of allowing individual businesses to benefit from someone's loss. The theory is that if property is lost, the general public should benefit from the use of that property until the true owner can be found, rather than letting one individual business reap the benefit of a windfall that does not actually belong to them. "Finder's keepers, loser's weepers" definitely does not apply! Meanwhile, the state is allowed to audit businesses to ensure that they are not hoarding property that does not belong to them.

Once the state has recovered the unclaimed funds, it is charged with safeguarding the assets for the true owner. The reason that states are so willing to go after these "lost" assets on behalf of their citizens may be the fact that states can invest that money and keep all of the interest earned without ever having to pay the extra money earned to the true owner, if or when they come to claim it. The state is even permitted to charge an administrative fee to the true owner, which the owner must pay to recover his or her own property (on which the state has been collecting interest), and can require the true owner to jump through multiple paperwork hoops to prove that he or she actually *is* the owner of the property. No wonder only about 20% of the abandoned property held by the state is ever successfully claimed by the true owner! Most of my clients have found their *own* unclaimed property listed on some state's Web site while trying to bring their companies into compliance. There is a Web site where 31 states list their unclaimed property all in one place; it's called www.missingmoney. com. Make sure that you check the site for your company's name and your own name.

TERMINOLOGY

First, let us address some terminology that may be unfamiliar to you. The most important term used in our discussion is *unclaimed property*. You will hear it called abandoned property, escheat property, and unclaimed property, but it all means the same thing: something tangible or intangible that the true owner has not claimed or exercised any powers of ownership over for a statutorily prescribed amount of time.

Another term that is bandied about is *holder*. What is a holder? Generally, it is the entity that is in possession of or has control over abandoned property until it is transferred to the state on behalf of the lost owner. This is usually the business that issued the property, but that is not always the case. When a company buys another company, for example, the acquired company's debts *may* become the obligation of the purchasing entity. In some cases, outstanding unclaimed property is transferred to the new company, along with the reporting obligation. You may be a holder without actually knowing it! We will talk about successor liability in Chapter 10 in the Mergers and Acquisitions section.

Another term to become familiar with is *dormancy period*. This is the period of time, according to state law, that must pass since the last date when an owner generated any action on their property. The dormancy period can be the period of time that has passed since the date that an uncashed check was written. It can be the last time that a savings account holder made a deposit, withdrawal, or inquiry regarding his or her account. The date of last contact by the owner, as listed in the records of the holder, is the date that states use to determine the start of the dormancy period for purposes of reporting unclaimed funds.

The term *activity* is important to our discussion as well. For our purposes, activity is action taken on a property *by the owner* of the property. It can include making a withdrawal, writing a letter or note to the holder regarding the property at issue, or even making a phone call, if the holder makes a note in their records. It is important to note that the action must be initiated by the owner, not the holder, to restart the dormancy period. Merely sending statements or other correspondence does not constitute activity, even if the mail is not returned by the post office.

There are several more important unclaimed property terms defined in the Glossary. If you are unfamiliar with any of the terms, just turn to the back of the book for a more extensive explanation of their meaning.

What Types of Property Can Become Abandoned Property?

Just about any type of intangible personal property can become abandoned. Common examples of property that can become abandoned include: financial institution safe-deposit box contents, money orders, traveler's checks, payroll checks, insurance settlement checks, utility deposits, securities, court deposits, mineral proceeds such as royalties and the underlying shares of mineral property, and many, many more items. Property can become abandoned when people die without leaving clear information about their assets, when people move without notifying companies of their forwarding addresses, or even when they marry or divorce and change their names. Companies merge, are acquired, go out of business, or just change their names. Businesses buy new software, and old information about outstanding checks is not transferred during the system conversions. People lose their savings account passbooks, stock certificates, and certificates of deposit. Grandparents purchase stock certificates or open bank accounts in the names of their grandchildren without ever telling those grandchildren about the gifts, and then die without leaving any documentation. College students move away from the cities where they went to school without leaving forwarding information for their utility companies. Sometimes, it is as simple as forgetting that we have something deposited somewhere. Our society is more mobile than ever before, and people sometimes lose track of their assets.

WHEN DOES AN ITEM BECOME UNCLAIMED PROPERTY?

Although there is no uniform set of unclaimed property laws that applies to all of the states and territories, the way property becomes abandoned is fairly uniform. Property is considered abandoned or unclaimed if it is (1) held in the ordinary course of a holder's business, (2) constitutes a debt or obligation of the holder to a creditor or owner, and (3) remains unclaimed for more than the statutory dormancy period. Let's break these requirements down:

- *Held in the ordinary course of a holder's business.* This means that the abandoned property is the kind that the business usually deals in. For example, a retailer typically pays employees through payroll checks, pays for merchandise to its vendors with checks, and pays its rent and utilities with checks. Employees and vendors may be paid through electronic funds transfers (EFTs) and direct deposits in the usual course of business. They may issue store credits to customers who return merchandise and sell gift certificates or gift cards. These are all done in the ordinary course of a retailer's business.

  A retailer might also make charitable donations in merchandise or in the form of a check. If the donation check is never cashed or the donated merchandise is never picked up, is it abandoned property? *Yes.* Is it subject to reporting under the escheat law? *Probably not.* Why? Charitable donations are not made in the ordinary course of a retailer's business. They are usually one-off transactions. We will look at other defenses to having to turn over abandoned property later in this chapter.

- *Constitutes a debt or obligation of the holder to a creditor or owner.* This means that the check or credit was issued to cover an actual debt of the business that issued the intangible personal property. For example, payroll checks are generally issued to pay an employee for the time that he or she worked. Sometimes, when employees quit or are terminated, payroll checks may automatically be issued for them, even though they did not actually perform the work. If you do not actually deliver a wrongly issued paycheck to a former employee, it appears to be unclaimed property on your books, but it is not actually escheatable because you did not owe that employee for hours they did not actually work. That incorrect payroll check would not be escheatable.

- *Remains unclaimed for more than the statutory dormancy period.* This is the easy part! Dormancy periods are the statutorily determined periods of time that transpire since the last date on which an owner generated any activity on his or her property. If it is in reference to an outstanding check, this period starts to run on the date the check is issued. For example, payroll checks in most states become dormant one year from the time that the check was issued. If the check was written on June 23, 2007, it became dormant on June 23, 2008. You simply have to be able to add your months and years together to know when to report.

It is important to know that reissuing a check to replace a check that is about to become dormant does NOT start the dormancy clock over again! A check is just a document representing the underlying debt created to the payee when the check is written. The underlying debt is the focus of the dormancy clock; not the date of the piece of paper. Exchanging one piece of paper for another (i.e., reissuing a check) does *not* satisfy the debt. If the new check is not cashed before the date that the original check would have become escheatable, then the amount *must* be reported on the date that the original check would have been due. We will discuss this subject further in Chapter 6 when we review Policy and Procedure Manuals.

When is property not considered abandoned? It is not unclaimed if the owner has increased or decreased the amount in an account, if there have been written communication with the holder, if the owner has indicated an interest in the property that is reflected by a memo or record in the holder's file, or if the owner has another relationship with the holder where there has been owner-generated activity. We will discuss these defenses later in the book.

So, you know what unclaimed property is and why you are a holder, but why do you have to report it to the state? Because the law says so. Both the states and holders have statutory obligations.

States' Responsibilities

Under the unclaimed property laws, states have some responsibilities once they have taken possession of the escheated property. First, they must release and indemnify the holder from liability. Once the holder has properly reported the abandoned property to the appropriate state agency, the true owner can no longer go to the holder to recover his or her property or any associated interest.[8] Second, the state must secure the funds in a custodial capacity, which means that the state has the fiscal responsibility to ensure that the funds are kept in a safe place or investment vehicle until they are recovered by the true owner. Third, the state must make efforts to locate the true owners. In many states, the law requires publishing the property lists in different state newspapers and making the lists available for public perusal at the state offices. Most states try to publish their lists on their Web sites or take lists to state fairs for people to review. More than 30 states list the unclaimed property in their possession on a Web site called www.missingmoney.com. Fourth, the states are required to pay claims. The states will require that everyone requesting unclaimed funds to be turned over to them present some proof of their ownership or right to claim the funds on behalf of the true owner. There may even be an administrative fee involved in processing a claim for an owner. All of these steps must be fulfilled before the state will return the funds owed to someone, but the state *will* give the money to the true owner eventually.

Holder's Responsibilities

The unclaimed property laws give the holders a lot of responsibility for trying to reunite the true owners of abandoned property with their assets. Holders have the obligation, under the law, to report any escheatable unclaimed property that they are holding to the states. Before that property is turned over, however, most states also require holders to perform due diligence or make some attempt to locate the true owner themselves. If a holder cannot find the true owner, the states require that holder to remit the property to the state for safekeeping. The U.S. Supreme Court has identified a method for holders to use to determine the state to which the property should be reported, and I will discuss this in Chapter 3. The states *all* have enforcement powers to provide incentives for holders to do their duty under the law. If the property is not turned over the state, the holder can be subject to late reporting and nonreporting fines and penalties, which can double and even quadruple the amount of money that the holder should have reported initially.

There are fines for failure to report and remit the unclaimed property. These usually accrue daily, for each day that a report is late. There are also fines and penalties for failure to comply with the statutes, including interest on the outstanding property at rates of 10% to 25% of the property value. There are civil, and sometimes criminal, penalties for failure to report and remit the property, or for filing a fraudulent unclaimed property report. In some cases, nonreporting and underreporting can lead to prosecution by other government agencies. Underreporting your company's unclaimed property liability and/or taking unclaimed funds into income on your company's books and records can have serious implications on the accuracy of your published financial statements. This can spell disaster under the new Sarbanes-Oxley Act. Implementing proactive internal controls and procedures will help reduce your company's unclaimed property reporting exposure and keep you out of the news.

Another aspect of the holder's obligations is the responsibility to keep the unclaimed property safe until it is either reunited with its rightful owner or turned over to the state for safekeeping. Holding unclaimed property can be more of a headache than you might think. This is also an area where some businesses are the victims of *fraud*. If businesses do not safeguard property for the true owner during the time that it is in their custody, the holder may *not* be fully indemnified by the state they report the property to. The true owner may have a cause of action against a holder who was negligent with the owner's property during the time the holder held it, causing the property to lose value. A good example is a bank that transferred funds from dormant interest-bearing accounts into non–interest-bearing accounts until they were escheated. Because the true owner lost the extra money from interest while the bank was still in possession of the funds, the former account holders might still have a cause of action against the bank, even after the funds were escheated to state care. It is important to recognize your responsibilities as a holder to both the true owners and the states. Otherwise, you risk costing your company money in a lawsuit.

Unclaimed property is frequently the target of internal and external fraud. Because it is historically ignored by many companies, their outstanding unclaimed property can be a very tempting unsupervised area for the few employees in the know. Employees can siphon unclaimed funds away from a company for years before anyone notices that funds have been misplaced. Outside parties could set up elaborate schemes to pretend to be the rightful owners and claim unclaimed funds belonging to other people. If your company is the victim of unclaimed property fraud, you will have to pay the funds *twice*—first to the fraudster and second to either the true owner or the state! In fact, your company can become the subject of a civil lawsuit brought by the true owners of the property if you did not safeguard it properly against fraud. We will delve more deeply into avoiding unclaimed property fraud in Chapter 10, Selected Legal Issues in Unclaimed Property Audits. Having specific and thorough claims procedures and internal controls can help prevent fraud from costing you more than you actually owe in an unclaimed property audit. We will address the development of these essential unclaimed property policies and procedures in Chapter 4, Calculating Your Company's Unclaimed Property Liability.

NOTES

1. *Dictionary.com Unabridged* (v 1.1), s.v. "Escheat," http://dictionary.reference.com/browse/escheat (accessed November 25, 2007). Based on the *Random House Unabridged Dictionary,* Random House, Inc. 2006.
2. Michael Houghton, Walter C. Tuthill, Josiah S. Osibodu, Valerie M. Jundt, and Mark A. Paolillo, *Unclaimed Property* (BNA Corporate Practice Series, 2006), p. A-7. (hereinafter *Unclaimed Property* BNA 2006.)
3. Ibid., p. A-8.
4. *Texas v. New Jersey,* 379 U.S. 674 (1965).
5. *Unclaimed Property* BNA 2006, p. A-8.
6. Ibid., p. A-10.
7. Ibid., p. A-7.
8. The holder may not be indemnified, however, if he or she does not handle the abandoned property correctly under the law while it is in his or her care. We will discuss the issue of indemnification in Chapter 6, Developing Unclaimed Property Policies and Procedures.

CHAPTER 3

Basics of Unclaimed Property Reporting

You have discovered that unclaimed property laws exist, and someone in your company has deemed that it will be YOUR job to bring the company into compliance. What do you need to know to get started? Start with the Holder Questionnaire in Appendix A. It will direct you to the places where unclaimed property might be hidden in your company. Next, read this chapter for the who, what, when, where, and why of a properly run escheat compliance program.

WHY YOU MUST REPORT YOUR UNCLAIMED PROPERTY

We will start with the *why*—because it is the law! As mentioned earlier, all 50 states, the District of Columbia, Guam, Puerto Rico, and the U.S. Virgin Islands all have unclaimed property laws on their books. Unclaimed property reporting is *mandatory,* not voluntary. States are becoming very aggressive in seeking out nonfiling companies, especially when those companies are registered to do business in their states. Not only do the auditors look to see if companies are filing, but they check each type of business against similar entities in the field to see if they are reporting the types and amount of unclaimed property typical for their line of business. Unclaimed property administrators are also training auditors from other state administrative disciplines, such as sales and use tax and income tax, to recognize unclaimed property reporting problems during their routine audits. To stop penalties and interest from accruing against your company, you need to get into compliance with state unclaimed property laws.

Determining Your Liability

The next step is *what*—what types of abandoned property is your entity holding? Check your answers to the Unclaimed Property Holder Questionnaire; did you identify any previously underreported property types? You can get some more ideas from reviewing an unclaimed property report. Most states have these blank reports available on their Web sites. Pay close attention to the list on the back of the form called the property classification table. This list is a good place to begin determining what types of abandoned property your company could be holding.

Some property types, such as payroll, are typical for many different businesses, but some property types are specific to certain types of businesses. Here is a list of just some of the types of unclaimed property for some common entities:

Corporate

- Accounts payable or vendor checks
- Wages/payroll
- Untendered stock certificates
- Untendered bonds
- Uncashed stock dividends and bond interest checks
- Unpaid retirement account distributions
- Accounts receivable credit balances
- Unidentified cash/miscellaneous income
- Abandoned tangible personal property
- Self-insurance benefit payments

Retail

- Layaway accounts
- Gift certificates/gift cards
- Rebates

Banks and Financial Institutions

- Checking accounts
- Savings accounts
- Matured certificates of deposit or savings certificates

- Christmas Club accounts
- Unidentified deposits
- Suspense accounts
- Safe-deposit box contents (tangible and intangible personal property)

Insurance/Non-Life Insurance Companies

- Individual policy benefits/claims
- Group policy benefits/claims
- Proceeds due to beneficiaries
- Premium refunds
- Unidentified remittances
- Other amounts due under polity terms
- Agent credit balances

Utilities

- Customer overpayments
- Customer deposits
- Royalties

Oil and Gas

- Royalties
- Mine shares from closed and abandoned mines or wells that have been reopened

Manufacturing

- Accounts receivable credits for merchandise spoilage/returns
- Accounts payable credits for damaged/spoiled supplies
- Shipping weight adjustments/credits

This list is not exhaustive, but we will address some of the compliance issues related to certain industries later in Chapter 8.

There are exemptions for certain types of property under some state laws. Some commonly exempted items are gift certificates, gift cards, credit memos, business to business transactions, and tangible personal property. While these exemptions are not universal, they are quite common and can reduce your unclaimed property compliance burden if applied properly. We will discuss the specifics of these exemptions in Chapter 7.

WHERE YOU MAY HAVE A REPORTING OBLIGATION: JURISDICTION

Once you have determined the outstanding funds for your target year, your next step is identifying *where* those funds may need to be reported. The U.S. Supreme Court determined the pecking order for unclaimed property reporting in a 1965 case called *Texas v. New Jersey*.[1] While the facts of the case are really interesting to unclaimed property attorneys, the outcome of the case is all you need to know. The U.S. Supreme Court established Rules of Jurisdiction for reporting unclaimed property to prevent more than one state from making a claim against a holder for the same property. The Primary Rule is that property escheats to the state of the payee's last-known address according to the company's books and records. The Secondary Rule is that if the payee's address is unknown, the property escheats to the company's state of incorporation. For example, X Company, which is incorporated in Delaware, has a plant in Cincinnati, Ohio. X Company had an employee, Sam Snow, who gave his address as 123 Poplar St, Covington, KY 41011. When Sam Snow quit, he asked the company to send his last paycheck to him. The company sent the check to 123 Poplar St, Covington, KY, but it was returned by the Post Office. Apparently Mr. Snow had moved without notifying X Company of his change of address. After the statutorily prescribed period of time, X Company must report the unclaimed property. They are bound to report the property to Kentucky, Sam Snow's state of last residence, according to their records. If, however, Sam Snow's address has been lost in X Company's last system conversion, they would have to report the unclaimed payroll check to Delaware, their state of incorporation. Ohio, the state where their plant is located and where Sam Snow worked, gets no part of these unclaimed funds.

What if you have an address that is incomplete or that you know is wrong? If you know that the address is wrong, but you do not have a more current address, you should still report the property to the state of the true owner's last known address. Things become a little trickier if the address is incomplete. The states' concern is that for an address to be complete, it needs to be usable by the U.S. Postal Service. Missing zip codes or apartment numbers and even incorrect street names can be corrected by the U.S. Postal Service under most circumstances. Missing cities or street names make it almost impossible for the Postal Service to deliver an item of mail. If you *at least* have the state of the owner's last known address, you should report the property to that state. If you do not have the state, you should just default the property to your company's state of incorporation when it comes time to report. Incomplete true owner addresses also make it impossible for your company to perform due diligence on those items.

Due Dates, Due Diligence, Aggregates, and Dormancy Periods

One of the most important aspects of a successful unclaimed property compliance program is making sure that outstanding unclaimed items are reported to the states in a timely manner; this is the *when*. In the majority of states, unclaimed property reports are due on *November 1*. The November 1 report for any year covers property that became reportable (meaning its dormancy period expired) during the period of July 1 of the prior year to June 30 of the current year. A handful of states have alternate annual report due dates, such as May 1 in Tennessee, which covers all of the property that became dormant during the previous calendar year of January 1 to December 31. Insurance companies also usually have a report date all their own, which is typically May 1, when they report all of the property that became dormant during the previous calendar year. This industry is specifically addressed in Chapter 8, under Special Industry Considerations.

Dormancy periods vary by state and by property type, but they are generally defined as the period of time that must elapse before property is considered unclaimed and reportable. The average dormancy period is three to five years, but it can be as short as six months and as long as fifteen years. In most cases, the property you report in one year was probably issued three to five years previously.

Before you can report your company's dormant property to a state and relieve yourself of the burden of keeping track of it, you must first attempt to contact the true owner of the property and give them one last chance to claim it from you. This is called *due diligence*. Each state has its own unique set of requirements, some more burdensome than others, but you are generally required to send a first class letter to the true owner at the last known address you have for them, according to your company's books and records.

Many states have attempted to relieve some of the administrative burden that your business must bear for smaller-value abandoned items. If you have no address for the true owner, or the property is below a certain dollar amount in value, you can skip the due diligence step. If you have an address, but know it is bad because you have had previous mailings returned by the U.S. Postal Service as undeliverable, you can also skip sending a due diligence letter to the known bad address. This process is burdensome and costly for most companies and yields very few responses, but it is just one of the steps your company must complete to be in compliance with the law.

There is some small measure of relief to be found in the statutes in the form of aggregate reporting. If an item is valued at or below a certain de minimis amount of money, you do not have to attempt to find the actual owner before you turn the funds over to the states, and you do not have to give any of the detail for that item on your unclaimed property report. You just lump all of these small amounts together and turn them over. The average aggregate amount is $25, but it is as much as $100 in some states. We will discuss this topic more in Chapter 6 in the section on aggregates.

PREPARING THE REPORT

Now, *how* do you actually file and prepare your unclaimed property reports? You may be able to prepare them by hand or electronically, using software. You can do it in-house or outsource to an unclaimed property professional, but the information required will be the same. Generally, the reports require a specific list of information for each item to be escheated (assuming that the items are larger than the aggregate amounts). You will need to report your holder contact information and your holder identification number, which is typically issued by the state, but is also sometimes the entity's Federal Employer Identification Number (FEIN). You will need the owner's contact info (name, address, Social Security number/FEIN), the property type to be reported, the date that the property was originally issued or created, and the amount of each item. While much of the information requested will be the same, each state will have subtle differences in what they request to be reported.

The best way to learn how to prepare your unclaimed property reports is to *read the instructions* for all of the state reports you must prepare! In this modern age, unclaimed property reports and instructions can be found on the states' Web sites, but if you would like to receive a copy directly from the state, you can contact their respective unclaimed property offices for a holder report. The contact information for the various states can be found in Appendix D. The instructions for preparing the unclaimed property reports for the respective states will give you vital information such as:

- Does the report need to be filed electronically?
- Must payment be made electronically?
- Who must sign the report?
- When and how should you remit the property?
- Is a negative report or a zero report required?
- What property codes are associated with the property our company needs to report?

You may have only seen paper reports, but some states *require* entities that meet certain criteria to file their reports electronically. There are several methods of filing unclaimed property reports electronically. Some states, like Ohio, have "one-click" filing for negative or zero reports. Most states' Web sites offer a free software package that can be used to create unclaimed property reports on electronic media. However, any holder can report electronically, as long as the files are in the accepted National Association of Unclaimed Property Administrators (NAUPA) format. NAUPA is a nonprofit organization made up of state unclaimed property administrators, with the goal of creating a central resource for legislative and enforcement issues. Their standard reporting format has been accepted by almost every state. NAUPA is currently working on a standardized, simplified list of property reporting codes that, they hope, will be accepted by all state unclaimed property offices. Following the NAUPA format can make your compliance burden a little lighter.

This is the most basic information that you will need to properly report your company's unclaimed property every year. We will be delving into the specifics of these matters in the chapters ahead. You know where to start; now we will get you into compliance!

NOTE

1. *Texas v. New Jersey,* 379 U.S. 674 (1965).

CHAPTER 4

Calculating Unclaimed Property Liability

Y ou know what unclaimed property is and why companies have to report it to states. You know that your company has outstanding unclaimed property and is probably not in compliance with the law in every jurisdiction. Maybe you have been reporting *everything* to your state of incorporation for the last 15 years. Maybe you only reported accounts payable and payroll, but you know that you probably have accounts receivable credit balances that should have been reported to several state unclaimed property divisions. Maybe your company has *never* filed . . . Where do you start?

To come into compliance and report properly, you need to know what you owe and to whom it needs to be paid. You start by auditing your own company. Whether you have received your first audit notification letter or you are just trying to bring your company into compliance voluntarily, you need to *become your own auditor!*

GATHER YOUR RECORDS

The first thing that you need is an accurate list of *all* of your company's accounts. You will need to review each account separately to find the outstanding unclaimed property in each of them. I have included in Appendix E a sample Audit Records Request that is typical of the list of documents you will be requested to gather for an unclaimed property audit. The list is long, but it is exactly what an unclaimed property auditor is going to demand when they contact you for the opening conference of your audit. You will have the advantage over an external auditor because you know your company, how it works, and who to ask/bug/harass for the information you need. Initially, you should concentrate on gathering as much information as you reasonably can. Make a note of the information that cannot be found or can no longer be accessed from your old software or your company banker's box hoard at the local public storage. We will address record reconstruction and projections later. First, learn what you have. We will worry about what you do not have later in the process.

Identify Your Company's Unclaimed Property Types

Your next step is to determine the types of abandoned property that your entity is holding. You can get an idea of your property types by reviewing any unclaimed property report and the holder questionnaire discussed earlier. For our purposes, if you have been contacted for an audit, concentrate on the lead audit state's laws. If you are doing a self-audit, work from the rules of your state of incorporation first. We will address your nonincorporation state liabilities later in the process. Most states have blank reports available on their Web sites. Review the form to understand the information that you will need to gather. Pay close attention to the list at the back of the form, called the property classification table. This list is a good tool to use to determine what types of abandoned property your company could be holding. If your company has unclaimed property that may be exempt in some states (e.g., gift certificates), it is important to calculate the liability for this property anyway; it may *not* be exempt everywhere your company is required to report unclaimed property. We will discuss exempt property later in the book, but make sure that you account for *all* property at this early stage in your self-assessment.

Determining Your Liability

Now that you have some idea of the types of outstanding unclaimed property that your business may be holding, you need to determine how much actual abandoned property you owe to the states. You should start by collecting the documentation that an auditor will ask for if you are selected for audit. Gather the following:

- Corporate structure
- Current chart of accounts
- General ledger trial balances

- Annual reports
- Policy or description for handling outstanding, undeliverable, and voided checks
- Unclaimed property reports previously filed
- Prior unclaimed property audit reports
- Outstanding check report (bank statements) of all disbursement accounts (e.g., accounts payable, payroll, dividend, expense reimbursement)
- Voided check register (including stop payments)
- Accounts receivable aging report
- Journal entries of amounts written-off or charged-off (except for bad-debt write-offs)
- Description of Third-Party Administered programs (TPAs)

Now that you have all of the information, or know what you are missing or cannot easily retrieve, you can start to calculate your company's liability. The corporate structure and chart of accounts will help you determine all of the possible sources of outstanding unclaimed property in your organization. Some entities, especially holding companies, will probably not generate *any* unclaimed property and probably have very few, if any, operating accounts, while others will generate quite a bit.

Once you know which entities are generating potential unclaimed property, you need to understand how outstanding items are being handled. Some companies leave outstanding checks on their books indefinitely, waiting for the item to clear. Other companies write off these outstanding items annually, making journal entries to document the trail of money. Still others just void checks and take the money back into income. Whatever approach your company takes, you need to know how to track the outstanding funds. If you are audited, you will find out that states are not only concerned with how the paper is handled, but are more interested in the underlying debt that prompted the creation of the check or credit on a company's books.

Why do you have to pull up a list of every outstanding item on your books? The law assumes that, if your company took the time to write a check or create a credit on your financial records, then an underlying debt must have existed between your company and the payee/credit holder. Until that underlying debt has been satisfied by having that check clear your account or having that credit offset on your financial records, the state considers the originally created obligation to pay, represented by the check or credit, to be unclaimed property. Explained simply, every time you write a check, you create unclaimed property. That property is "claimed" when the check is cashed by the payee. If the check is never cashed, and you cannot prove that the underlying debt was satisfied in some other way (i.e., the customer forgave the debt or negotiated a different payment amount), then you owe that amount of money to the state upon audit. The same theory holds true for stock certificates, payroll checks, and safe-deposit box contents, to name a few items of potentially reportable unclaimed property. I describe it as a "guilty until proven innocent" approach to administering the law. You must show all of your outstanding unclaimed property, and then you will be given an opportunity to show why it is not reportable. The auditor will demand to see everything, so you need to review everything as well.

Unclaimed property audits typically cover a period of ten to fifteen years, although they can go back to the date that your company opened its doors for business under most state laws. To make audits "reasonable" to complete, most states limit their look-back period to ten report years. For our purposes, let us assume that your Voluntary Disclosure Agreement/audit will be negotiated to cover that length of time. This means that the property you are looking for would have been due to the state during the last ten years. The property might actually have been created much longer ago than that, though, because property is not reportable until its dormancy period has passed. The dormancy period for payroll checks is typically one year, and the average dormancy period for vendor checks is three years, but the holding period for traveler's checks is fifteen years! If your business issues traveler's checks, you may be reporting checks in 2009 that were actually issued in 1994! Those records will be tough to find for most businesses.

To quickly determine just how exposed your company is to an unclaimed property liability, I would suggest picking a recent fully completed fiscal year and calculating your amount of outstanding unclaimed property for that one period. Multiply that amount by ten (for ten report years). This will give you a decent idea of how much your business might owe for the entire period that it might be at risk for an unclaimed property audit. While this one year will not provide you with information regarding all the jurisdictions to which you may owe unclaimed funds, it will probably give you a general idea of how much you will owe to your

state of incorporation, as opposed to other states. As your state of incorporation is the most likely to audit you, you must gain a good understanding
of where you stand with this state in particular. It is also very important to
remember that all of the property for which you do not have associated
addresses will, by default, be claimed by your state of incorporation. If you
do not maintain name and address information for your outstanding
unclaimed property, you will owe it all to your state of incorporation.

Check all of the reportable unclaimed property types that your company has generated and make a list of the exposure items you find. The
industry averages state that checks are generally cashed within 90 days of
issuance. If they have not been cashed after 90 days, they will most probably never be cashed. If your company has a policy of voiding checks
after six or twelve months, you need to review all of the checks that have
been voided that were issued within your target period. Find out how
many outstanding payroll checks you have at the end of each year. Do
not concern yourself with trying to identify the reason that the items are
outstanding right now—just determine the raw numbers.

One important thing that I typically see underreported by my clients is
property that is contracted out to TPAs, such as payroll, securities, and
cafeteria plan administration. Unless you have specifically contracted with
your TPA to track and file unclaimed property reports, they are probably
not filing unclaimed property reports on your behalf. You should contact
your TPA immediately to find out how it handles returned checks,
uncashed checks, and direct deposits that are bounced from the bank. If
they are filing unclaimed property reports on your behalf, ask to have
copies sent to you. Ask for a copy of their policies and procedures related
to uncashed and returned checks. Their policies may not be in line with
what the law requires. If the TPA is returning a list of uncashed checks
and bounced deposits to someone in your company, follow up with that
person to see how these returned items are handled internally. Too often,
I see my clients putting these lists into a file without ever following up
on the outstanding checks and deposits for unclaimed property purposes.
This can be a big area of exposure for your company after a few years,
especially since the dormancy period for payroll checks is typically only
one year from the date the check is issued.

Besides the collection of all of this data, you also need to gain a good
understanding of how your company has dealt with unclaimed property

in the past, on a department-by-department basis. If your company is small, you will probably know who to ask down the hall. If your company is large, this task may be a lot more difficult. How are returned checks or bounced direct deposits handled? How long does the accounts receivable department leave credits on the books for stale customers? Do customers with a credit balance have to request a refund check, or does your accounting department automatically issue one after a certain period of time has passed? Does payroll automatically mail final checks to former employees, or do they just hold them until they are picked up? These are the types of questions you will ask to begin to understand your company's processes.

You will need to find all of your old unclaimed property filings (if there are any). Look at the void check registers to get a handle on voids that may have been unclaimed property rather than accounting errors. Ask the payroll department what they do with uncashed payroll checks or bounced direct deposits. If they outsource payroll, ask for contacts at the TPA to see how they are handling the issue for your company. Just finding outstanding checks may not be enough to determine your actual unclaimed property liability. If your company has been writing aged checks and credits off into income, you need to calculate those amounts into your figures as well; the auditors certainly will!

You Do Not Have All of the Records for the Audit Period: Determining the Best Estimation Technique for Your Company

You have hunted and gathered all of the records that you can. You realize that there are some gaps in your ten-year collection. To calculate your true escheat liability, you will have to find a way to fill in or reconstruct those gaps. Unfortunately, state auditors will not forgive you for losing track of amounts. Most states' unclaimed property laws specifically require companies to maintain unclaimed property records for an indefinite period of time or until you are audited, whichever comes first. You were not aware of this law? That's no surprise, but you will have to come up with a good way to estimate what your records might have shown as your reportable unclaimed property. Now is the time to channel your inner statistician!

What? You cannot find the channel that broadcasts your inner statistician? You lost that remote in your last system conversion? No problem; there are several generally accepted estimation techniques that unclaimed property administrators accept to allow auditors and companies doing self-audits to make an educated guess as to what their unclaimed property liability might have been for the "lost years." We will talk about them briefly, but I am not going to explain them all in detail, as I am not a statistician either! I will give you a general explanation that should allow you to make use of the science yourself. If none of these methods seem fair to your particular industry, or if you do not have the resources to do this yourself, you could also hire a statistician from your local university to design a model that is more reflective of your business model and what your liability might have been. As long as they use standard statistical sampling methodology (that you can explain to the unclaimed property administrator), your projections should be acceptable in lieu of actual records to the state administrators.

As an overview, the science of statistical sampling is based on the idea that the attributes found in a representative sample of a population can be proven to be an accurate reflection of the entire population. For example, when you are cooking, you might taste a small spoonful for seasoning. If the item is mixed well, you can assume that the spoonful you have tasted is a good representation of how the entire dish will taste. The science of statistical sampling takes this same idea and applies it to large bodies of objects or data. State unclaimed property administrators allow their auditors to take a sampling of records for your company and apply the results to your entire audit period to determine your liability when you do not have or cannot produce records for your audit period. You can do the same thing for yourself with a little understanding of how the process works.

There are basically two types of samples: (1) judgment samples and (2) statistical samples. Judgment samples are solely based on the judgment of the person conducting the sampling. For example, if you have one year's worth of invoices and you choose to look at only one month's invoices from that year to get an idea of your sales, you have used a judgment sample. The results may be an accurate reflection of the sales for your company's entire year, but there is no way to prove its accuracy other than to look at the entire year's invoices and see if the sample method and the projection were accurate. This is probably *not* the way that you want an auditor to review your records during an unclaimed property audit, but it may be a reasonable way for you to conduct a self-audit when you have limited internal resources and records are scarce or hard to come by.

When an outside auditor is conducting an audit, you want him or her to use a more objective and accurate sampling approach. The less subjective their methods, the more accurate they are liable to be. Statistical sampling results are considered, within the scientific community, to be more objective, as they use mathematical methods with results that should be able to be duplicated with very slight differences by more than one researcher. Statistical sampling, if done correctly, can even be successfully defended in court. It is important to remember, no matter what method of sampling that you chose to perform, the results can never be exact; however, the rate of error can be smaller if the appropriate method is chosen. For the methods to work, each item in the sample population has to be selected completely at random, and each item must have exactly the same chance of being chosen as any other item. Several data selection techniques can provide this randomness. However, before the data is chosen, you need to develop a sampling plan.

You want to narrow down the parameters of the data universe used in the sampling process, meaning you only want the sample drawn from a specific group of information or data. Let us say that you have been notified of a ten-year audit period of July 1, 1998 to June 30, 2008. You only have complete records for the period of July 1, 2002 to June 30, 2008, so you will only draw your sample data from this group of records. If you know how big your data universe has become, you can decide how many sample items to choose overall. You can consult one of the standard data selection tables to help you choose a required sample size, or you can, again, consult with a statistician to help you pick an appropriate sample size.

Here are the five generally accepted selection techniques for choosing which items of data will be reviewed. *Random number sampling* chooses items from the entire population of data completely at random. For this to work, items all have to have some identifying number, like an invoice number or check number, so that each and every item has an equal chance of being chosen for the sample. There are several different published tables of random numbers that can be used by auditors to compile their random sample to analyze. The auditor will choose items from the data pool that coordinate exactly with numbers from the random number tables and will continue to choose items until the predetermined required sample size is met.

With *interval sampling,* each item in the data pool does not have to have some identifying number. The auditor selects items from the population of data so that there is a distinct and certain interval between each sample item selected. For example, an auditor may choose to look at every 50 items in the population of data. The auditor will pick a number between 1 and 50, or even draw a number randomly from a hat containing pieces of paper numbered from 1 to 50, to start the sampling process and will then look at every fiftieth item from that point on.

A *stratified sampling* is typically used when there is some sort of diversity between the types of data being researched so that a random or interval sample would not actually work for example, when items have a big range in dollar value. Some companies issue a lot of rebates that are small in value, but also issue a lot of vendor payment checks which are significantly larger. With a stratified sample, the auditor would split the population of checks into two categories, like refunds and vendor payments, and then take a methodical sampling of each. This will make the results a lot more accurate.

Cluster sampling is usually chosen because records for the entire audit period are difficult to get to or are really voluminous, so that reviewing every item would be a timing nightmare. All of the items that would make up the audit population are divided into groups or "clusters," and clusters are chosen at random to sample. For example, if a company keeps all of its vendor checks by vendor, and not chronologically, it would be very difficult for an auditor to sort through all of the vendor files looking for invoices for the period of time that the audit covers. They may choose to divide the vendors alphabetically and examine several letters of the alphabet instead of the entire vendor population.

Another method to keep in mind is *mechanized* or computer-generated sampling. With the movement toward totally paperless environments, computer programs can be created to randomly choose records and produce samples with the touch of a few keystrokes. These mechanized samples remove the judgment and any chance for human error from the process and are a good alternative to manual record review.

While the method of choosing sample items is important, remember that we are ultimately interested in the *results* of the sampling. Just getting these rough numbers is the beginning. The sample has to be analyzed within the framework of your business and how it operates to ensure that the information gathered will give an accurate picture of how your business handled its unclaimed property throughout the entire audit period. Remember that this sample will be compared to some static information that is available for the entire audit period, such as your gross or net revenues for the audit period, your sales for the audit period, or even the total number of checks and the average value of those checks issued during the audit period. The projected amount due can be vastly different, depending on which sampling method is used and what static values it is compared to.

When you are choosing a sample method for your self-audit, or working with the auditor to choose the sampling methodology that works best for your business, you have to look at factors other than just the volume and availability of your records. The daily operation of your company can have quite an impact on the results that each method can produce. For example, if you are a seasonal business, you would not want an auditor to use cluster sampling for fear that they would pick your busy months and not gather data from the months when your business is down. You certainly do not want the unclaimed checks from your busiest month in ten years to be projected across your entire audit period! This would present very skewed estimates.

If you have changed data systems during the audit period, or if you have had a lot of employee turnover with some records being kept better than others, you will want to factor this into your sample choices and into the limits you put on the pool of data from which your sample is drawn. If the numbers from the sample seem high to you, challenge the sampling methodology. It may not have been the right approach for your particular circumstances.

While this explanation of statistical sampling is cursory at best, it is important to know the basics of how an auditor will reconstruct your records if they are missing or unavailable. It is an important safety guard for you to know how to *audit your auditor*! No one knows how your company functions better than its employees, and the auditor does not have your bottom line's best interests at heart. Knowing how to test the validity of a sampling methodology can save your company thousands of dollars during an unclaimed property audit. You will also want to be familiar with how to best recreate your liabilities if you are performing a self-audit for purposes of a Voluntary Disclosure Agreement. Knowing how to conduct a proper internal test of your procedures can provide a valuable resource for spot-checking your compliance in the future, as well. You can save time and resources by executing a well-matched sampling of your records, rather than waiting for a full-blown audit to spot any compliance problems with your unclaimed property reporting.

Statistical sampling is all the rage in unclaimed property administration across the country. While it has the benefit of causing your company less time and hassle during audit, states encourage statistical sampling audits because these audits enable the auditors to perform more audits more quickly. Most states actually prefer statistical sampling projections, since the money comes into their coffers with no strings attached. As there is no particular owner associated with estimated property, there is little to no chance that anyone will ever claim that money from the state fund. The government will be able to use the interest, and in some cases the actual property, for its own purposes, albeit for the common good of the state's citizens.

The flip side of using sampling and projection methodology is that the numbers are just guesses and are probably more than your company would have had to pay if it had the authentic accounting records. Sometimes, records are just gone, or the data is so difficult to mine that the time spent by your staff or your consultants would be *more* expensive than the projection.

To see if a sampling methodology might actually save your company money during an audit, you can do a test run. Take the total unclaimed property you actually owe from your most recently completed report year and then compare it to a sample projection method or two run using the data from that report year. If the estimate numbers are very similar (or even less than) your actual unclaimed property due for that period, it may not be worth the time spent excavating deeply buried boxes of paper or translating old data files. Keep in mind the method that provided the most accurate projection, as compared with the actual unclaimed property that your company owed for the test period and make a note of it for future reference. You can always negotiate with an auditor or a state administrator to use a projection method that is proven to provide more accurate results for your particular business. Go with the projection and vow to do a better job of keeping your company's funds from becoming escheatable in the future.

Do Your Due Diligence

You have a list of your actual outstanding unclaimed property that either (1) already passed its report date or (2) is rapidly approaching escheat day. It is sorted into report states under the *Texas v. New Jersey* reporting standards. It is still not too late to perform due diligence. We discuss due diligence in detail in Chapter 6 and will go into specifics then. For now, just know that you need to attempt to contact as many true owners as you can to eliminate some of the outstanding funds that your records reflect as reportable escheat property, whether it is by issuing them a replacement check or having them sign something stating that you do not owe them anything. Most people are honest and will not claim money that does not actually belong to them.

Once you have whittled the list down to owners that you cannot find or resolve the unclaimed matter with in any other way, make sure that you actually have to pay the money over to the state unclaimed property departments under the law. Check the list in your policies and procedures manual for all of the statutory exemptions to reporting the property, such as business to business exemptions or gift certificate exemptions, in the states where the property should be reported first under *Texas v. New Jersey*. If the property is statutorily exempt in the first priority reporting state, next make sure that your state of incorporation does not claim it. If the property cannot be removed from your list of reportable property under a statutory exemption, try to eliminate it under one of the administrative exceptions, like the current business relationship or credit offset defense. If it is still on your list after all of these steps, chances are that you are actually going to have to pay the money over to a state unclaimed property reporting agency. It happens to the best of us!

Complete the Final Summary Report and Pay the Money!

For the items that remain on your list, prepare to pay the correct reporting agency. If you are under audit, the auditor will assess you. If you are going the Voluntary Disclosure Agreement route, start contacting the states where you owe money. We will discuss reporting property under a Voluntary Disclosure Agreement more in Chapter 5, Preparing for and Managing an Unclaimed Property Audit, but you should start with your state of incorporation. As your incorporation state is the one that gets the windfall of any unknown or "no address" property on your records, they will be most interested in speaking with you! If your incorporation state is not the state that contacted you for audit, contact it *as soon as possible* and ask to enter into a Voluntary Disclosure Agreement. If you do not call them, the state auditing you will!

You know what you owe and to which states you owe it. Now you can defend your audit, get into compliance with the states that have not contacted you, and design some policies and procedures to help eliminate as much future unclaimed property creation for your company as possible on a go-forward basis. The next couple of chapters will guide you through both of these phases.

CHAPTER 5

Preparing for and Managing an Unclaimed Property Audit

While it may not come as a surprise to anyone in the banking or financial services industries (which have been audit targets for more than two decades), many states typically concentrate their auditing efforts on specific industries that they feel are most noncompliant with unclaimed property laws. The states started targeting banks in the 1980s and have done their rounds in the insurance industry, financial services industry, the Fortune 500, and announced at an Unclaimed Property Professionals Organization National Conference in 2007 that they were aiming their audit guns at the automobile dealers across the country.

AUDIT TARGETS: ARE YOU NEXT?

State administrators have admitted to cross-referencing Secretary of State charter lists against unclaimed property report filers and putting all non-filers located within their states on an audit list. States check merger and acquisition news for audit targets. They drive through areas looking for signage to indicate previously unidentified businesses that might owe them outstanding unclaimed funds. What does this mean to your company? It means that you *never* know when you might get that audit letter in the mail! The chances of being chosen for an unclaimed property audit are pretty good. Your company's position in the audit game can make a difference in how much your unclaimed property compliance will actually cost.

Offense—Contact the States for a Voluntary Disclosure Agreement

If you have not been contacted by a state auditor, you can avoid some penalties and interest by contacting states where you might have an unclaimed property reporting obligation *first*. This could make your business eligible for a *voluntary disclosure agreement (VDA)*. A voluntary disclosure agreement is a contract between you and a state administrator in which your company or your company's representative performs a self-audit and reports past-due unclaimed property to the state administrator without paying extra penalties. Some state administrators even have the authority to waive interest payments that would otherwise be due along with your overdue unclaimed property. A VDA will usually limit the look-back period for the audits to ten report years or less. You will also get the benefit of explaining record discrepancies or unusual company policies or procedures according to your own deep understanding of how your company works, instead of depending on the limited understanding and assumptions applied by an outside auditor. Voluntary self-audits can also be administered with a more relaxed timeline than you would operate under within a state-initiated audit framework, in most cases.

Not every company will be eligible for one of these agreements, however. If you have received an audit letter from a state, you will not be permitted, in most cases, to perform a self-audit. A few states have a formal amnesty program requiring that your company has never filed unclaimed property reports in their states previously to qualify for penalty and/or interest waivers. This does not necessarily mean that you cannot be granted some quarter, however. If you are a past filer who has become delinquent, or a current filer who has discovered a problem with underpayment in your unclaimed property reports, it does not hurt to call the state administrator (anonymously) to explain your position and request permission to come into compliance without paying penalties or interest. Most state administrators have the discretion to allow this, but you have to ask—they do not just make random offers of safe harbor anymore!

VDAs can be handled by your company directly, or you can get outside consulting assistance, just as with any other audit. Consultants can also provide you with the shield of anonymity from state unclaimed property officials until you are ready to reveal your company's liability by entering into an agreement, with you named as an "unnamed holder" during negotiations. This can help protect your company from the loose tongues of any state employees or bounty-hunting third-party auditors who might attempt to contact other states regarding your noncompliance before you have a chance to do so. The anonymity can also help stave off any negative publicity that might follow news of an adversarial audit leaking out to your customers, your shareholders, or the general public. Since you pay your consultants by the hour, and not on a contingent fee, they will only be interested in getting the best outcome for your company. Your consultants are motivated to find and report only the unclaimed funds that are truly reportable to the states, rather than just turning over every outstanding item on your company's books like a bounty-hunting third-party audit firm might do.

Beware the Gift Horse

There is one unsavory element that I need to caution you against. Several companies might approach your company and offer to get you into unclaimed property compliance "at no cost to you." They claim that they will review your company's books and records and give you an estimate of your company's outstanding unreported unclaimed property, with no obligation on your part to continue with their services. After they tell you what you owe, they offer to report all the overdue property to the appropriate states and get you into compliance without costing your company a dime! This solution sounds too good to be true, because it is! It is important to understand that these companies actually work for *the states*. The companies do not charge you any fees because *the states pay them* a percentage of whatever they recover! They have no incentive to investigate the sources of your outstanding property to ensure that it is actually abandoned; they just "clean up" your outstanding unclaimed checks and credits by reporting *everything* to the states. This approach ensures that their payday is as big as it can be.

Even more uncouth, if, after seeing the amount of money that the auditing company claims your company has underreported, you decide that your company does not want to continue with the VDA process, the auditors leave, but they put on their whistle-blower hats and report you to the states as nonreporters! In fact, the same auditors may be right back at your door with a state-assigned audit notification to force you to report—and they still get their commissions.

When you are shopping for an unclaimed property professional to assist you, check into their backgrounds very carefully. Ask the company representative if the company currently does any work, or has ever done any work, for any state unclaimed property office. Some groups have incorporated their state contract audit division separately from their holder consulting division, but they share common ownership and *all holder information* among their divisions. Ask them if they are part of a corporate family that has a state-associated audit division. Ask for references of past and current clients. Make sure that they are completely independent of any connections to state offices, or you will never be certain that they are only representing *your* company's best interests. A truly independent consultant will know *exactly* why you are asking these questions and will happily discuss all of their past and present associations with you. Those of us that have declared ourselves "holders-only advocates" are proud of this fact.

Where to Start

If you are just starting the VDA consideration process, keep in mind that you should contact your state of incorporation *first*. They are the most likely state to audit you and will probably be the state to which you owe the most outstanding unclaimed property, as they get all of your unknown and no address property under the current reporting priority rules established in *Texas v. New Jersey*. The states that you should contact next, if not contemporaneously, are states where your company's headquarters or any large facilities are located. If you are conducting business in a state, you are probably registered to do business there and your company's name will come up on an unclaimed property administrator's target list sooner rather than later. Other states to which your company may owe money but has very few obvious ties should come next on your list to contact for VDAs.

If you have been contacted by one state (or several) for an audit and you know that you owe money to still more states, contact those states as soon as you can. You can avoid the audit hammer in those places, at least! While it may seem like you are just offering yourself up to the slaughter, if you have outstanding unclaimed property, the penalties and interest alone can double and even triple the amount that you would pay if the states contacted you for an audit. The savings are worth it.

The process of conducting a self-audit for unclaimed property should be conducted in much the same way that you would handle an external audit.

Once you or your representative contact the state, you will usually receive a self-audit agreement and you will discuss a timeline for reporting; any estimation or sampling methods that you will be using; and the way you will remit payment. The state will communicate their expectations about performing due diligence; the documentation they would like you to provide to support your self-audit findings; and the way they would like your audit findings delivered to them (i.e., electronically on disk, over the Internet, or in hard copy). The state may request that you submit separate reports for the past years, just one summary report for all of the years, or only your audit findings. You and your representative should keep in periodic contact with your assigned state audit liaison to keep them apprised of the audit's progress and to ask any questions as they arise. You will proceed with your self-audit in the same way that you would prepare for an outside audit—by gathering data and recreating missing information as carefully as possible.

DEFENSE—YOUR COMPANY HAS RECEIVED NOTIFICATION OF AN AUDIT: DO NOT IGNORE THE LETTER!

So you have received a letter from a state unclaimed property office. It may or may not be an audit notification letter. Several state administrators have been sending "gentle reminders" to businesses that they believe *might* have an unclaimed property obligation in their state. They may be sending your company a letter because you have filed in the past, but have not filed an unclaimed property report in the last few years. Maybe you have acquired a company that used to file, but you have not kept their filings up to date; or maybe you bought an ongoing business that some state has had its eye on for years, and you are the unlucky successor owner who actually receives the unclaimed property enquiry. You could have gotten the letter simply because some state's division of unclaimed funds has decided to give holders a chance to get into compliance by letting them know that *they know* you exist and that you *might* have an obligation to file an unclaimed property report in their state. This may be one step short of an actual audit notification letter. You may still have a chance to contact the state and enter into a VDA before an audit is initiated. If the letter you receive does not clearly state that you have been chosen for an unclaimed property audit or "examination," there may still be some hope of avoiding an audit.

Even if you believe that your company owes the particular state that contacted you nothing in unclaimed funds, you should *not* ignore the letter! You can give them a call to let the administrator's office know that you received the correspondence and ask what initiated the letter. Whatever the answer, communicate that your company is aware of its responsibilities as a holder and actively monitors its unclaimed property liabilities. Follow your conversation up with a short letter confirming that you have received their letter and are aware of your potential reporting obligations, but that you do not owe any unclaimed funds to their state at this particular time; assure them that you will turn any future reportable funds over to them in a timely manner.

If you believe that you *do* owe that state overdue unclaimed property, ask the state representative about the availability of an unclaimed property voluntary disclosure program. If they have enough information to send your company a letter regarding unclaimed property, they have enough information to initiate an audit of your books and records. Even if they are not auditing you immediately, they will put you on an audit list if they do not receive any response from you regarding their outreach efforts. Take the initiative to save yourself the money and headache of an adversarial audit— start the voluntary disclosure process.

If you have, indeed, received the dreaded audit notification letter, it may read something like this:

> The State Administrator of Unclaimed Funds of [State] has noticed that you have not been reporting unclaimed funds to [State] and would like to send an auditor to review your records to determine whether you have inadvertently underreported escheatable funds that may be reflected in your books and records for the last ten report years, covering the period of July 1, 1998 to June 30, 2008. Please have the following (inexhaustible) list of records available for our review by [six weeks from date of letter].

If you have received a letter with some variation on this theme, then you know what it is to be chosen for an unclaimed property audit. Before the auditors arrive, there are several acts of damage control that you can perform to (hopefully) limit the impact of the audit on your company's bottom line.

Audit letters come in a variety of forms, but they are generally issued by the state's unclaimed property administrator's office and will usually list an employee of the auditor's office for you to reference as a contact person. Some will list several states that will be auditing you at the same time. Some will include the name of a third-party audit firm that the state has hired to review your records as their representative. You may also receive a call from the auditor's office to let you know that a letter is on the way or that you should have received their notice of audit letter by now. Make a note of the name and number of the state employee who contacts you, as you will become very familiar with that person as your audit progresses.

Once you have been notified that your company has been chosen for an audit, you need to start your audit management preparations as soon as possible. If you do not feel that you have the internal resources or knowledge base to defend the audit yourself, now is the time to call in a specialist to represent you during your audit. The more time the consultant has to prepare you and your staff for the audit, the better your outcome should be. The consultant can begin working with you and your staff to gather the records that will be requested by the auditor and get a handle on your potential unclaimed property obligation before the formal audit begins. They can also contact the other states, such as your state of incorporation, before the auditors arrive.

First Contact

The more you know about your company's unclaimed property obligations before the auditor arrives, the better prepared you will be to limit the assessment to the least amount of cash outlay possible under the law. If they have not already called you, you and your consultant should contact the auditor assigned to your company as soon as you can to let them know that you received the letter and you are interested in managing the audit process as efficiently as possible. If applicable, introduce your consultant and let the auditor know that a specific person will be the contact for your company during the audit process. Early communication will demonstrate that you are cooperative. By giving the state audit staff a specific contact person and letting them know you have brought in a professional to make sure your company's interests are well represented, you will be starting off on the right foot with the audit staff. If the state auditing you has assigned a third-party contractor to your audit, ask for signed copies of the authorization form assigning your company to the contractors. You have a right to be given proof that the contractors are actually authorized by the state to audit you and to see the terms under which the contractors will be paid for the audit. If the contracting firm has had some dealing with your company in the past, such as being your former auditors or tax preparers, ask for a state employee to be assigned to your case to avoid any conflict of interest or prejudice based on the audit contractor's knowledge of your business.

You should also take this opportunity to establish the scope of your audit. Some states will list the audit period in the notification letter that they send you. Others leave that important bit of information for the opening conference. If you do not have a stated audit time period in your notification letter, ask the audit contact that is assigned to your case to identify the time period involved. If they give you an audit period, request that they state that time period in a short letter and send it to you. If they will not write a letter, compose a short letter yourself and request that the lead auditor or audit supervisor sign the letter and return it to you for your records.

If your auditor does not seem willing to discuss the time period involved, write a certified letter to the state unclaimed property administrator and request that your audit be limited to ten report years, covering the most recent report year and the nine previous report years. A ten-year audit limitation is a reasonable request and is the average length of time that most audits cover, so your request should be granted.

The initial call with the auditor would also be a good time to discuss a confidentiality agreement to be executed between the state, any third-party audit personnel and your company. Many states offer them as a matter of routine, but if the state auditing you does not offer, ask if they will provide one for your records. If the state or states auditing you do not have a standard confidentiality agreement, have your legal counsel draw one up to be signed by the state administrator or unclaimed property audit supervisor, any auditors reviewing your records, and any third parties that might be involved. The importance of the confidentiality agreement is twofold. First, you want to limit this involuntary audit to as few states as possible, and you do not want this lead state or group of states, or their bounty-hunting contractors, to report any outstanding unclaimed property you may have to other states before you can contact them voluntarily. This would take away your opportunity to avoid penalties and interest in other states by negating your eligibility for a VDA with them. Second, it is important to have the state agree to safeguard your important financial information, especially if there are potential Health Insurance Portability and Accountability Act (HIPAA)[1] ramifications for information that might fall into unauthorized hands. It may be necessary, if there is potential unclaimed property within very sensitive records, for the state to agree that you be given extra time to "desensitize" records provided for purposes of this audit. This is certainly a topic that you should discuss with your legal counsel if HIPAA issues apply to your company.

The initial call with the auditor would also be a good time to ask for an extension of the start date or opening conference of your audit for a reasonable amount of time to get your records together. If you ask for an extension of time of between three and six months, your request will probably be granted. If you have some specific logistical issues, such as out-of-state record storage, now would be the time to bring it up. Some states will cancel your audit if your records are not located within their state limits. This is an exception, but it is worth mentioning if it is, in fact, true that your company's records are not within the auditing state's boundaries.

Recruit Your Team

If you have not been successful at having your audit cancelled, and the state was not intimidated enough by your vast knowledge of unclaimed property law to decline to challenge you, you must prepare your staff and your records for the upcoming battle. You have to think like an auditor and know what information they are seeking if you want to to gain the advantage for your company in the upcoming series of battles that will make up your unclaimed property audit war.

To fight this battle successfully, you need to muster your troops. Gather a key group of your company's personnel to make up your audit team. Ideally, the team should include a representative of each department that might be holding unclaimed property for your company, such as payroll, accounts payable, accounts receivable, treasury, and human resources, to name a few. These departmental representatives will collect information for the audit. If your company has a legal department or outside counsel, you may want to add them to the audit team as well. Each member of your audit team needs to understand that this audit is serious and could potentially be very costly to the company.

You may be wondering when, if ever, you should bring your legal department or legal counsel into this process. Notify your legal department of your audit as soon as you get the letter. If they have any knowledge of the unclaimed property area, they will be a good addition to your audit team. Even if they have no legal expertise in this specific area, they should follow the progress of your audit to ensure that they are fully prepared to litigate any legal issues that cannot be resolved. As we will discuss in the Appeal Process section later in this chapter, the appeal process for unclaimed property assessments is informal, or even nonexistent, in most states, so you may have to instigate a lawsuit to fight your assessment if things go badly. The sooner your attorneys know what may be coming, the better prepared they will be. They can also help with the formation of company policies and procedures for handling unclaimed property in the future.

Know Your Enemy: Unclaimed Property Auditors

To prepare yourself for an audit, it helps to know as much as possible about your auditor. Many states employ a staff of dedicated unclaimed property auditors whose sole job is to audit the books and records of assigned companies for compliance with the state's unclaimed property laws. For this, they receive only their salary, no matter how much or how little underreported unclaimed property they recover while auditing a company. They are usually well versed in their state's laws and have a good understanding of how administrative policies are applied. They are usually given some amount of authority to make decisions regarding audit issues and will answer directly to their state administrator. They have no financial interest in the outcome of your audit, but they are generally spread thin and have many audits going at the same time. Their schedules may not be as flexible as you might like, but they try to be reasonable.

Several states, because of a lack of personnel or funds, are authorized by their state's laws to hire third-party auditors to perform unclaimed property audits on the behalf of the state. These third-party auditors are *not* state employees and are usually (although not always) compensated based solely on a percentage of the amount of unreported unclaimed property they "find" during an audit. Their average rate of compensation is 12% of what they "recover" for the states. It is likely that they are working on behalf of *several* states and will audit you for property under-reported to 15 or 20 states at one time. Some of the large national audit-ing firms, like NAPPCO (National Abandoned Property Processing

Corporation), Kelmar and Associates, Audit Services Limited (ASL), and ACS Unclaimed Property Clearinghouse, have contracts to actively audit on behalf of as many as 30 states or more.

There is a lot of controversy surrounding third-party contingent fee auditors, or "bounty hunters" as they are unaffectionately known around the unclaimed property world. Holders and consultants (like me) who have made a commitment to represent *only* holders feel that there is an inherent conflict of interest in hiring a company that has a financial stake in the outcome of an audit to perform this type of service. Many holders have challenged the constitutionality of contract auditors performing these services. None has been successful at keeping auditors out, up to this point. Even more egregious, most of these firms also represent holders, or purport to, against the state! As discussed earlier in the chapter, these companies are working both sides of the fence, and you cannot tell where their allegiances lie, even if you are paying them. Despite the legitimate objections that holders and holder advocates have raised, these contract auditors are permitted by most states to audit on their behalf (at least for now).

States also work in cooperation with other state agencies within their own governments to train personnel to look for unclaimed property during the course of their other audits. Sales and use tax auditors, income tax auditors, and regulatory auditors are all being versed in their state's unclaimed property laws and looking for underreported funds during their routine audits. While these personnel might not know all of the subtleties of the unclaimed property laws, they will certainly know enough to spot obvious underreported property and pass the information onto the appropriate unclaimed property office personnel. While you may not automatically be made aware of the problems they see, you will probably be notified of a further audit by the escheat office if they deem it necessary.

Because of a lack of resources, many states also work cooperatively with each other to share their own personnel in the States National Audit Program (SNAP). A SNAP audit will typically include a review and assessment for several different states, but the auditors conducting the investigation are state employees with no financial interest in the amount of the final assessment. While it will be a larger assessment than you would have with a single state audit, it will not be driven by a commission, as would an audit conducted by bounty-hunting third-party auditors.

It can also be insightful to know how your auditors will be preparing for this audit. If your auditor is a state employee, he or she will most likely be reviewing the state's standardized audit program. Almost every state has one, and they rarely vary by more than a few points. Auditors start by evaluating your business type and comparing it to the list of typical property types that will be found in a company like yours. They will review any of your previously filed unclaimed property reports to see whether you historically filed all of the appropriate property types and whether you reported amounts of unclaimed property commensurate with other businesses in your industry. They will provide a list of targeted questions and personnel whom they will attempt to interview to gain insight into your company.

When a state auditor comes to your offices, he or she will be looking for various pieces of information to build the case that will defend your assessment to their superiors. The auditor will want to establish your company's historical level of compliance with unclaimed property laws, both in their state and in others. He or she will consider your internal control to judge whether you are actually managing unclaimed property carefully and according to the law and will want to look at any internal policies or legal opinions upon which you are basing your company's unclaimed property compliance positions. The auditor will want to establish that you are maintaining normal levels of compliance during the audit period—if you are suddenly ramping up previously lax efforts, the auditor may consider that a sign that your past compliance will need further investigation. State auditors are paid by the hour no matter what the outcome of your audit, so they will be preparing for a general overview of every aspect of your business and of areas where unclaimed property might be underreported. If your auditor is a member of a SNAP audit team, they will be familiarizing themselves with the laws of the multiple states involved, coming up with lists of questions, and targeting property types to search for.

If your auditor is a third-party contingent fee auditor, he or she is probably preparing a little differently. As these auditors are not paid by the hour but are usually compensated by a percentage of the unreported unclaimed property that they find in your books and records, they are concentrating more on the property types that other companies in your industry are reporting in large volumes. The auditor will not concentrate on small-dollar items, since those will not bring the biggest bang for their consulting buck. They are also happy to use estimation techniques, since they usually result in inflated assessments, so they will be boning up on their statistical sampling skills. It is likely that third-party auditors will not follow any state's standardized audit program and will likely be auditing you on behalf of several states, so the auditor will be researching the reportable property types, dormancy periods, and laws for the states involved.

AUDIT TIMELINE

The audit process has begun, and you can expect it to be broken into several phases. The audit timeline is basically made up of the following steps:

Step 1. Notification
Step 2. Records request
Step 3. Opening conference and site visit
Step 4. Records analysis
Step 5. Assessment
Step 6. Exit interview
Step 7. Appeal process

Records Requests

Even before your opening conference, the auditors will send you an extensive list of the documents that they want to review as part of your audit. As we mentioned earlier in the book, the list of documents will probably include most, if not all, of the following:

- Chart of accounts
- General ledger/trial balances
- Annual report
- Journal entries
- Bank reconciliations
- Voided checks/void check registers
- Credit balances
- Organization chart
- Unclaimed property policies and procedures
- Miscellaneous income/expense accounts
- Transfer agent data
- Employee benefit plans
- Past unclaimed property reports

The auditors will want to review these records for all of the years involved in your audit. Chances are, if you are like most companies, you will not have all of these records for the entire audit period. Most companies have a record retention policy of seven years, which coincides with the statute of limitations for federal tax audits. This will not help much with the unclaimed property audit, however, since the records at issue will probably cover the past ten years plus the amount of time for the dormancy period of your underreported property, which is probably another three to five years on average.

As you gather records, make sure that you make note of the records that will not be available, either because they are older than your company record retention policy or because they never existed. These are the items that may have to be reconstructed or be the subject of estimation techniques later in the audit process.

Opening Meeting

The opening meeting will be the first time that your audit team is face-to-face with the auditors. While it is important to be as pleasant and professional as possible to establish a good rapport, it is vital to set ground rules early in the process so that you can control the progress of your audit. You will want to discuss the procedures that the auditor proposes to follow during the audit. Ask if the auditors have a standardized audit procedure and, if so, ask for a copy. The more familiar you are with how they will approach your staff, the better your audit team can prepare.

This meeting is a good time to discuss an audit timeline. How long do the auditors expect to be onsite and during what hours? Ask for a copy of the auditors' work plan. How long do they expect record reviews to take and when should your company expect to receive some preliminary findings during their record review process? Communicate with the auditors about the progress (or problems) with retrieving the records they requested. Determine a reasonable time for you to retrieve or attempt to reconstruct missing records. If you know there are records you will not be able to provide, this meeting might be a good time to talk about estimation techniques and statistical sampling. Because of our discussion in Chapter 4, you are familiar with sampling techniques and you may have even run a few against your records to see which types would bring the most accurate results for your business model. Talk with the auditors about what you know, and ascertain their position regarding sampling techniques. You may have to set a specific time for a meeting with the audit supervisor or unclaimed property administrator if your audit team and the auditors cannot come to a meeting of the minds in this area. Even if you cannot resolve the matter entirely, it is good to begin this discussion as early in the audit process as you can.

Discuss any administrative issues, such as whether auditors need badges to be on site and to whom they are permitted to talk or approach without your audit team's permission. Discuss a schedule for interviews that might need to be conducted. Show the audit team where you have provided work space for them while they are onsite. At the end of your opening conference, your auditors may begin their actual review work, if there are records available to them, or they will set a date and time for their return to begin the business of the audit.

Site Visit and Records Analysis

While the auditors are on your premises, they are collecting information for their audit workpapers. Everything they observe can impact your final assessment. Besides just making note of the financial information that you are providing to them, they will observe your offices and learn how your company records are kept to determine whether the data you provide can be trusted. They have lists of questions to ask your personnel to determine whether you have proper internal controls. They will make subjective observations about how cooperative or secretive your personnel appear to be. They are gathering evidence that will support their audit assessment.

Once the auditors have gathered the information that they need, they will either copy it or take the copies you have provided to them and continue their analysis off site. Make sure that you keep a record of *every* document or copy that you provide to the auditor. Whenever practical, provide the auditors with copies of records, rather than originals, for their review, even on site. Do not let them take original documents off site. If your records are damaged or destroyed, there will be no way to recreate them and defend your audit.

This phase of the audit can stretch over several different site visits and last from a few weeks to several months, depending on the amount of actual records that you can provide for the auditors to review. It is no mystery what they are doing all of this time; they are finding all of the property in your records that appear to be unreported unclaimed property, and they are making a list of it.

After the audit team has completed its initial analysis, it will usually complete a draft report of examination. You should request that the auditors provide you with a copy of this document as soon as it is completed so that you can begin to understand where the audit is going and clear up any misconceptions early in the audit process. Review the auditors' analysis closely for any errors and do any research that you need to exempt as much potentially reportable property that you can before the items on the assessment become *final*.

The draft report of examination will be in three parts. The first part is the *scope of the examination*, which talks about the types of property covered by the audit and the period of time included in the examination. This section may also discuss any *reinstatable property*, or property that the holder determined to be exempt from reporting, but which the auditors feel should be included in the assessment. The second section will discuss the *exam procedures*, including any statistical sampling and estimation techniques that the auditors had to use in the absence of actual records for the audit period. The third section will be the *exam findings*—the unclaimed property items and amounts that the auditors feel your company underreported. It will probably list the apparently reportable items by property type and will discuss any legal positions that relate to the property listed.

It is important to remember that this report is just a *draft;* you will still have an opportunity to refute the auditors' findings.

Closing Meeting

This meeting is the culmination of the auditors' visits to your company and will likely be the last site visit that the auditors make to your facility. You and your audit team will meet with the auditors to discuss their observations and findings about your company's unclaimed property obligations. If you have not already received a copy, you will be presented with a draft report of examination during this meeting. You will also likely get a preliminary assessment.

Hopefully, if you have hounded the auditors to get you a copy of the preliminary report before the meeting, you will have a lot to discuss. Take the time during this meeting to read through the draft report and challenge the auditors on anything that appears to be incorrect or incomplete. Make sure that you completely understand the basis of any estimation techniques they may have used. Get a copy of all of the workpapers that the auditors have used as a basis for the assessment, if you do not already have them. Now is the time to challenge anything that you can reasonably challenge, before the audit assessment becomes *final*. Ask the auditors to explain the appeals process to you in detail. This process may not exist for some or all of the states under this audit, but if it does, you will need to know how to manage the appeals process.

If you can put the closing meeting off until you have had time to refute some of the items in the preliminary report (including proof for your refutations), you can provide the auditors with your findings during the meeting. While the auditors probably will not agree to make changes on the spot, make note of the topics discussed so that you can follow up later. At this point, the auditors will discuss the next steps in the audit with you, including the length of time you have to challenge any or all of the assessment, the types of proof you will need to provide, and the date by which any proof of challenge must be provided to the state before the audit becomes final.

Final Assessment

This is the final explanation of your audit findings—and it is, essentially, your bill. It should not be a surprise to you if you have been actively managing your audit process. Hopefully, you have been able to whittle the preliminary assessment total down to a reasonable amount. If you have provided any information to refute findings in the draft report of examination, hopefully this final report will reflect them. The final assessment letter will come from the state unclaimed property administrator, not the auditors. It will give you final instructions, such as whether you need to complete an unclaimed property report (manually or electronically) and how the state would like the funds to be submitted (e.g., check, wire transfer, etc.). They will also give you a date (probably around 30 days) to complete these tasks.

For better or worse, because of the lack of unclaimed property appellate laws or policies, this is probably the end of the road for your audit. Your audit period will officially be closed by the state unclaimed property office and you will officially be indemnified by the state against claims by any true owners against you for the period of this audit. You have three choices: (1) pay and move on, (2) refuse to pay and wait to be sued by the unclaimed property administrator, or maybe (3) appeal your final assessment (if an appeal process is available).

Appeal Process

The appeal process may not exist for your audit. Unlike the extensive and well-established laws surrounding your right to appeal any tax assessment, most states have little, if any, formal procedures for filing an appeal of an unclaimed property assessment. Even the few states that do have appellate procedures in place, such as Ohio[2] and Oklahoma,[3] will not always inform you of your options. You may think that your only alternative is to pay the assessment or refuse to pay and file/defend a costly lawsuit. This is not always the case.

Some states, like California[4] have an administrative regulation (not codified law) that allows an aggrieved holder to request an informal review of the auditor's findings as soon as the exit interview has taken place. Other states, like Ohio,[5] require that you wait until after you have received your final assessment to file an appeal and only allow you to appeal to the director of the division of unclaimed funds. If you do not find the relief you are seeking, you may have no recourse short of filing a lawsuit and challenging the state government in a court of law. This is a potentially costly undertaking and should be avoided except as a last resort.

Unless you have discussed your appeal options during the exit meeting or have been given specific instructions in your final assessment letter, you will probably have to call the state unclaimed property administrator's office to inquire about your ability to appeal any aspect of your final assessment. You can also bring your legal counsel in to do research as to your appeal options. Formal appeals processes in the unclaimed property arena are virtually nonexistent. Many states have no formal process for appealing an unclaimed property assessment, but there may be informal routes that you can take to have your assessment changed, short of filing a lawsuit.

You may be able to request a meeting with your auditor's supervisor or the director of the unclaimed funds department to discuss changes in your assessment. Maybe you will have to approach the State Attorney General's office. Just as there are no formal rules for appealing, there are no formal rules prohibiting the unclaimed property administrators from changing a final assessment. They have wide discretion in their offices. Sometimes, all you have to do is keep asking them to use it. It is also important that you have some basis for requesting your changes. Maybe new records have been found that prove some apparently unclaimed items were not actually outstanding debts. Maybe the extrapolation method used for your business was too aggressive and does not accurately reflect what you should be paying. Believe it or not, most unclaimed property administrators that I have dealt with have been very reasonable people. You may be surprised at their willingness to work with you. If you get nowhere with the informal approach, and your state's administrators are not willing to work with you, you will have to either pay the assessment or file a civil lawsuit to have the matter investigated further. Remember, even if you choose to file a lawsuit, it's probable that you will still have to pay the assessment first and hope for a refund if your litigation is successful. If you refuse to pay, every state has powers to forcibly collect funds through the court system (as part of their audit powers). Either way, you are going to be writing a check, either to your attorney or to the state administrator, and you will still be obligated to file your unclaimed property reports on a go-forward basis.

AUDIT BEST PRACTICES

You know that any audit is painful. It costs your staff time and distracts them from their regular duties. The best way to minimize the damage that an unclaimed property audit will cause is to manage the audit process as closely as possible. Nail down the states involved in the audit as soon as you are notified that you have been chosen for an unclaimed property review. Organize your internal audit team and quickly assess your potential unclaimed property exposure, both to any audit states and to states where you have not yet been identified as an audit target. If you know that you have underreported property past due to other states, contact those states as soon as possible to start negotiating a VDA, and especially with your state of incorporation if that is still an option. If you have been reporting property to any states, continue with your normal unclaimed property reporting practices. Do not ramp up your efforts just because you are under audit; you may actually be doing things correctly. Remember that some audits reveal that you do not actually owe any outstanding unclaimed property!

Make sure that you understand the scope of your audit and develop a timeline with the auditors. Have a clear agenda for your meetings with the audit team and with the auditors, and make sure that all of the involved parties have contact information for each other. Check in with the auditors periodically to make certain that the timelines you have established and the deliverables that you are to provide to each other are on track. The more involved you are in the front-end of the audit investigation, the less surprised you will be by the final assessment.

You and your audit team must carefully document the delivery of any and all information to the auditors. Consider any potential confidentiality issues and discuss their ramifications with your legal counsel and the auditors before you turn sensitive information over to anyone. Try to get the auditors to sign a confidentiality agreement before you begin handing over the information they request. If you are active in the audit and not just an observer, you will get the best outcome that you can expect given your prior history of compliance with unclaimed property laws. It may be painful, but your audit will not be as costly as it would be if you just give the auditors free rein to draw up a list of every outstanding check, credit, and unidentified remittance on your company's books and records for the past ten or more years!

Post-Audit Cleanup

Once the dust from your audit has settled, it is time to plan for the changes that need to take place internally to prevent your company from ever having another outstanding unclaimed property assessment levied against it. You will need to develop thorough unclaimed property policies and procedures to ensure that you account for, perform the legally required due diligence for, and correctly report any and all unclaimed property that your company may create from now on. You will not be able to completely eliminate your unclaimed property reporting burden, but you can certainly pare down the amount that you will actually have to report. All it takes is a plan.

NOTES

1. HIPAA refers to the Administrative Simplification provisions of the Health Insurance Portability and Accountability Act of 1996 (HIPAA, Title II), which required the Department of Health and Human Services (HHS) to establish national standards for electronic health care transactions and national identifiers for providers, health plans, and employers. It also addressed the security and privacy of health data. (From www.hipaa.org, a Web site administered by the U.S. Government Department of Health and Human Services).
2. See Ohio Admin. Code §1301:10-3-04 *et seq.*
3. See Okla. Admin. Code §735:80-1-4.
4. See *California Guidelines for Requesting an Informal Review of an Unclaimed Property Examination* (Sept. 1999).
5. See Ohio Rev. Code Ann. §169.03(F)(7), which states that "any holder of unclaimed funds may appeal the findings of an audit . . . to the director."

CHAPTER 6

Developing Unclaimed Property Policies and Procedures

By now, you have gathered all of the information you can find on your company's unclaimed property. You think you know how much you owe and where it should be reported. Next, you need to chart a course to put your company into compliance with unclaimed property laws and keep them there in the future. Establish company rules and give your employees easy steps to follow to meet those requirements by adopting an *Unclaimed Property Policy and Procedures Manual*. Establishing a complete and straightforward set of unclaimed property policies and procedures for your company will give you what every company wants: a firm hold on your unclaimed property compliance.

You might ask why it is important to have written policies and procedures in place. The answer is simple: *It makes your company's unclaimed property program easier to administer*. Every department will know exactly what to do with the unclaimed property created by their everyday activities. Responsible parties can quickly begin to investigate potentially abandoned items, which can substantially reduce the number of items that have to be escheated in the future. Besides, just as a cake is much easier to bake with a clear recipe, any program is easier to administer properly with a clear set of procedures in place.

When developing a set of unclaimed property policies and procedures for your company, no matter how large or small, the first part of the manual should declare your company's commitment to ongoing compliance with the unclaimed and abandoned property laws of all jurisdictions to which you may become liable. Employees have a lot of company policy changes thrown at them, and it is sometimes hard to discern whether a new policy is really meant to establish permanent change or is just a management attempt to fill a paper void identified by an internal auditor. They need to know that you are *serious* about unclaimed property compliance.

The reasoning for this declaration of intent is twofold: First, anyone who picks up the manual will understand that unclaimed property compliance is mandated by law and that your company is aware of its legal responsibilities and is making every effort to meet the law's requirements. Employees and auditors need to understand that unclaimed property compliance is not just an optional program initiated by your company to promote customer relations or to overburden already extended department members. *It is the law.* Have the commitment section signed by a high-ranking corporate officer or, in a smaller company, by the owner to show that the commitment comes from the top of the business chain of command.

Second, this statement of commitment can become even more important when you are chosen as an audit target. When you are notified that your company is scheduled for an unclaimed property audit, the auditors will ask to see your policy and procedure manual in their initial document request. Having this manual readily available and having your intention to be compliant clearly stated will give your auditors the impression that they are dealing with well-informed professionals who are probably compliant with the law already. They will be predisposed to give your company the benefit of the doubt on questionable items if they believe that you are making every effort to meet the law's requirements.

As you develop your policies and procedures for unclaimed property administration, it is important to include a set of instructions for each of the departments that may be involved in collecting information about, tracking, or administering any potentially escheatable property created by your business. If your company is small, there may only be two or three individuals who will contribute information, but a large company could need hundreds of people who actively track potentially reportable property. Ideally, an oversight committee made up of a fiscally responsible corporate officer and a member of each of the different reporting segments of the company should be formed to ensure that your entity's policies and procedures are being properly administered. You can make provisions for the formation of this committee in the Intent section of your policies and procedures manual.

This committee approach will help ensure that no one person is left with the overwhelming task of tracking all of the unclaimed property created by your business. It will also guarantee that the person who collects unclaimed property information is not preparing the reports and paying out any claims. Members of the committee can spread the responsibility evenly and make sure that any new employees or committee members have the benefit of experienced tutelage and are not just left to fend for themselves in unfamiliar territory. This extra set of eyes can also reduce the risk of unclaimed property fraud in your company, which we will discuss more in Chapter 11.

To prevent "unclaimed property fatigue" and help prevent fraud, different parties should be responsible for tracking and reporting unclaimed property. If possible, a neutral party should double-check the work done by the committee. Checks and balances ensure not only that your company's compliance is done properly, but also that no fraud is being committed against your company that will have to be paid for at a later date. We will discuss more about how to prevent unclaimed property fraud, both by employees and outside parties, in Chapter 11, but know that having property disappear from your control because of fraud is not a defense; you will have to pay it all over again to a state when you are audited!

The departments that most commonly need to be involved in unclaimed property tracking and reporting are payroll, accounts payable, accounts receivable, and employee benefits. Depending on the size and nature of your business, however, you may have unclaimed property information coming from the treasury department, the shareholder relations division, shipping and receiving, safe-deposit box administration, membership services, and others. Each department that will be feeding information to the group preparing the unclaimed property reports should have a clear-cut set of procedures to follow. The policy and procedures manual should provide this guidance.

We have included sample policies and procedures in Appendix B to jump-start your own company's program. It may not be completely applicable to your particular business, but it will give you a good place to start. After you make your commitment statement, you should discuss some general guidelines that will be the same for every department. For example, the information that should be retained for true owners should be consistent across every department and should include instructions to retain only the information that your company would collect in the regular course of business. For example, if you collect employee and vendor addresses and Social Security numbers (SSNs) or Federal Employer Identification Numbers (FEINs), keep that information. If you do not normally collect name and address information when you sell gift cards, do *not* start doing so for unclaimed property administrative purposes. The law does not require that you collect extraordinary information for purposes of reporting unclaimed property, but it *does* require that you keep records of the information that you have collected in the course of your business relating to reportable unclaimed property for a certain period of time. We will discuss record retention requirements in more detail further on in this chapter.

After the generalities are laid out, identify each department involved in your compliance efforts and give simple directions about how each department should handle the outstanding items under their care. For example, tell them how often the unclaimed property oversight committee wants them to check their lists for outstanding items and what they must do with returned checks or bounced electronic funds transfers. Inform each department how often they should try to contact true owners and, specifically, how you expect them to document any ongoing contact with customers, vendors, and others, which could restart the holding period on potentially dormant property.

Exhibit 6.1 is an example from the sample policies and procedures manual in Appendix B relating to an accounts payable department.

The excerpt gives the accounts payable department all of the direction they need to properly handle any unclaimed property held in their department. They are given a specific time (*at the end of each quarter*) to start their investigation into any outstanding property (*each voided check and any check outstanding for 90 days*) created by their department, told where to send the information they collect (*tax department*), and given a deadline for delivering the information (*no later than 30 days after the quarter*).

You may even want to name one or two specific job title holders in each department who can be alternatively responsible for coordinating the delivery of the collected information when it is due. Having clearly defined responsibilities for a named position in each department will ensure that all of the company's unclaimed property knowledge is not

EXHIBIT 6.1   **SAMPLE UNCLAIMED PROPERTY POLICIES AND PROCEDURES FOR THE ACCOUNTS PAYABLE DEPARTMENT**

I.   **ACCOUNTS PAYABLE DEPARTMENT PROCEDURES FOR OUTSTANDING AND VOIDED CHECKS**

A.   At the end of each quarter, the following information must be forwarded to the Tax Department for each voided check and any check outstanding for 90 days. This information should be completed no later than 30 days after the quarter:

1. A copy of each bank reconciliation for the previous three (3) months
2. Enter each voided or outstanding check on a Microsoft Excel spreadsheet using the following columns:
    a. Number of owners on check
    b. Type of check (void or outstanding)
    c. Check number
    d. Check date
    e. Void date
    f. Owner's name (last name first)
    g. Social Security number or Federal Employer Identification Number, if applicable
    h. Amount of invoice before any deductions
    i. Amount of deductions, if any
    j. Net amount of check
    k. Mailing address (Street, Apartment/Suite)
    l. City
    m. State
    n. ZIP code
    o. Country, if other than United States
    p. Explanation of what happened to the checks, if void; if outstanding, is there still an open invoice to be paid with that member/vendor?
    q. Work paper number that will tie to the proper backup required

B.   Proper backup for a voided check
1. Copy of voided check
2. Copy of invoice or other source document that created the liability
3. A detailed description of the reason for the voided check
4. If duplicate payment, a copy of the new check
5. If paid to incorrect member/vendor, copy of the new check
6. If wire sent to member/vendor, copy of the wiring instruction
7. Any additional pertinent information

C.   Proper backup for an outstanding check
1. Copy of check
2. Copy of invoice or other source document that created the liability
3. A list of any invoices still open to the member/vendor
4. Information about any address changes in the past 90 days
5. Any additional pertinent information

solely located with any one employee or department and that employee or management turnover will not create an escheat compliance crisis in your business. Employees retire, quit, get fired, and go out for extended sick leave, but your company's unclaimed property compliance burden does not take a vacation.

To be effective, your policies and procedures manual should outline, step-by-step, what to do with the types of unclaimed property that could be handled by each department of your company. Payroll should have clear direction regarding bounced electronic funds transfers (EFTs) and uncashed manual payroll and expense checks. Treasury and shareholder services should have clear instructions for handling returned or outstanding dividend checks. For example, it should be clearly stated that proxy mailings need to be closely monitored, because their return could indicate a "lost" shareholder who should be flagged for further investigation. Accounts payable should have precise instructions on handling returned vendor checks or how to deal with credits that have been outstanding for six months or longer. Any documents in a language other than English need to be translated into English. If original negotiable instruments are lost or missing, the correct department must know how to issue an instrument bond. All documentation needs to be organized and easy for a new person to pick up and work with. If you are clear from the beginning about what information should be gathered, how often, and from whom, as well as to whom the collected data should be delivered, your unclaimed property compliance will be very smooth.

COMPLIANCE TIMELINES: DUE DILIGENCE, AGGREGATES, AND DORMANCY PERIODS

You have been diligently tracking your outstanding unclaimed property. Per your policy and procedures manual, your departments have done timely follow up, but there are still several outstanding items that cannot be cleared from your escheat sheets. You have separated the property by states, using the last known address that you have in your records. If you have no addresses, you have placed the property into the list to be reported to your company's state of incorporation. Now, you must do the required due diligence and prepare to report the property to the correct states' unclaimed property offices.

Each state has different due diligence requirements, but generally, your company will have to send a first-class letter to the last known address (according to your books and records) of the true owner within 60 to 90 days before you escheat the property at issue to the proper state. The required information that must be included in a due diligence letter varies from state to state. The state of California has the most stringent and lengthiest list of requirements for proper due diligence of any of the states. Their requirements include a specific size of font for certain language in the letter, certain statutory language that must be included, and other specific wording that needs to be used. Not every other state is as specific, but a few others, like Ohio, have clear direction regarding specific information that they want a holder to include in their due diligence mailings.

You cannot create one stock letter that will meet the requirements of every state, as the statutory language will be different for each one, but you can create a letter template for each state that you can use again each year. Start by checking the requirements for the states that you have already reported to or the states that are on your list of dormant property. Review the Report Instructions for each of these states to identify any specific due diligence letter requirements. These requirements will also be listed on most state unclaimed property Web sites.

Content of Due Diligence Letters

Many of my clients have asked me just how specific the references to the outstanding unclaimed property have to be in these due diligence letters. Do they need to include the specific dollar amount involved and a check number? You may be concerned that you could be tempting people that receive letters to claim funds from your company even if the listed owner is not actually owed any money or if you have the wrong recipient altogether. In my opinion, unless a state's laws require that you specifically include a dollar amount and/or a check number, you should generally leave the specifics out of the mailing. Instead, use general language, such as: "Our records indicate that we have issued you a check in excess of $XX.XX (state's specific due diligence minimum value) that has not been presented for payment." Ask the addressee to contact you regarding the outstanding check or credit. If a letter actually reaches its intended recipient, that person will almost always contact you to settle the matter, whether it is to confirm that funds are owed to them or to tell you that their records do not reflect any outstanding amounts. The due diligence letters are not really likely to open you up to fraud. Require that signatures be notarized. This will typically ensure that no identity theft is being perpetrated.

Another question that comes up a lot is *when* to send the due diligence letters. While the law in a few states gives a very specific timeline for sending due diligence mailings, most state unclaimed property laws just want the letters mailed out with sufficient time for the true owner to contact the business before the final reports (and the funds) are escheated. The latest you can mail a letter is between 60 and 90 days before the final report is due, in most jurisdictions, but there is nothing to say that you can't mail out a letter much earlier.

One interesting fact to note is that some states, like Delaware, do *not* require that holders mail due diligence letters. With 80% of U.S. corporations incorporated in Delaware, that is a *lot* of unclaimed property that falls into the void of one state's unclaimed property coffers without any notification to the apparent true owners. Just a thought. . . .

Timing of Due Diligence Mailings

As discussed previously, the sooner you attempt to contact a lost owner, the more likely you are to actually reach them and return their property without having to escheat it. If you have phone contact information, try to call the listed owner. If you do not get a response, send one of your stock due diligence letters to their last known address. The U.S. Postal Service will forward mail for six months after someone moves. If you try mailing between three and six months after outstanding property is issued, you have a much better chance of actually finding the true owner than you would by waiting until three or more *years* have gone by! I suggest that you mail letters out quarterly. If a letter is returned, make a note in your records. You will not have to perform due diligence again later, in most cases, if you know that the address you have is bad.

It is important that you keep copies (either actual or scanned electronic versions) of all due diligence letters to provide proof of your compliance efforts when you are audited. You need to keep also the returned letters, including the envelope with the U.S. Postal Service stamp, to prove that your attempted mailings failed to be delivered or were returned by the recipient for any reason. These mailings are part of the record retention requirements that holders must meet for unclaimed property compliance.

Many clients have asked me if a phone call or an email could be considered enough due diligence for them to perform under the law. At this point, actual mailings through the U.S. Postal Service are still required under state unclaimed property laws. Emails and phone calls are *not* enough notification to an apparent true owner before property is escheated. Keep the information, though; it can still be very useful for your due diligence process. In this highly technical age, people may move every three to five years, but they rarely change their personal email addresses. It is not even necessary to change your cellular telephone number when you change geographic locations anymore. You can use these contacts to request updated street addresses for apparent true owners whom you might have lost track of otherwise. While states require that due diligence letters be mailed using at least first-class postage, true owners can fax or email their responses to your company. Some states even have more stringent requirements for unclaimed property worth larger amounts. For example, in some states, if the minimum value of the outstanding unclaimed property at issue is worth more than $1,000, holders must mail the due diligence letters via certified mail. Make sure that you keep copies of all correspondence from these apparent true owners, though, whether in hard copy or scanned image, for your own protection under audit. You never know when an auditor may demand to see proof that the property you removed from your escheat list was done so properly!

Aggregates

The states have each established a separate minimum dollar value for unclaimed items that each property must meet before due diligence needs to be performed by holders prior to escheatment to government coffers. The average de minimis aggregate amount for unclaimed property is $50, and the trends keep the amounts going up, but the lowest amount that any jurisdiction provides relief for is Puerto Rico, with $1. If the items that your company is holding are not worth *at least* the minimum amount listed in the laws of the state that the property would otherwise be escheated to, you are *not* required to perform due diligence efforts on those smaller items, and you are *not* required to maintain the name and address information separately when you report the property. The states allow you to lump all of these small items together and aggregate them into one line item on your unclaimed property reports.

At first blush, it seems like this would be an administrative relief for businesses overburdened by the rigorous due diligence requirements under state unclaimed property laws, but this seeming relief may not actually assist you in handling your company's due diligence. It is important to note that each reporting jurisdiction (there are 54 in the United States) provides a different de minimis reporting amount. Some states even have different de minimis amounts for different types of holders or property. For example, in Delaware, the de minimis amount for financial institutions is $25, while the minimum for other holders is $50. This disconnect can make a very confusing chart for your unclaimed property personnel.

While it saves you a small amount on the administrative side, aggregation can actually *cost* your company money in the long run. When you do not maintain the name and address information for all your outstanding unclaimed property, you run the risk of over-escheating these small amounts. When someone contacts you for a replacement check or to have previously dormant credits revived, you will probably, as a courtesy, attempt to make these payments to customers, vendors, or employees who make these requests. Oftentimes, your largest vendors or oldest customers will have several outstanding checks and credits at any one time which, when added together, can represent a tidy sum. If you do not keep information about *all* of your transactions, you may escheat these smaller items as part of your aggregate pool, even after you have refunded the money or credits to the apparent true owners. The larger your organization, the bigger the loss that aggregation can cause.

Another reason not to aggregate is that any funds reported to a state without owner information can *never* be returned to the person that they truly belong to. Since returning property to its rightful owner is supposed to be the very reason that the unclaimed property laws were established in the first place, this aggregation policy seems to fly directly in the face of the nature of the law. However, if your sole purpose is to clean up your books as quickly as possible and to become compliant with the letter of the unclaimed property law, you can certainly take advantage of the aggregation policy. Make certain, however, that your written policies and procedures reflect this policy clearly so that information is still properly maintained for items above the stated de minimis value listed for each state. If you want to further simplify matters, do not aggregate. Some states, such as New York, have different aggregation amounts depending on the property type and prohibit some property types (namely securities) from being aggregated at all. Keeping track of the minimum aggregation amounts in every state for every property type can be very complicated.

Dormancy Periods

As mentioned earlier, a dormancy period is the statutorily determined amount of time that elapses between when an item of potentially unclaimed property is created and the time when it must be escheated to the state for safekeeping. All states have different holding or dormancy periods for different property types. For example, Rhode Island has a one-year dormancy period for wages, but has a fifteen-year dormancy period for traveler's checks. That is quite a range!

The most important thing that your organization can do to avoid penalties and interest in the unclaimed property reporting arena is to *report dormant property in a timely manner!* Keeping track of the changes in dormancy periods can be tedious, but it is less expensive than late payment penalties and interest. All states publish their dormancy periods on their Web sites and in the instructions for their unclaimed property reports. It is vital to check the listed dormancy periods in your policies and procedures manuals periodically to ensure that you are still holding unclaimed funds for the appropriate period of time. If your company invests in an unclaimed property software package, you will probably receive these updates automatically. If you do not, check my Web site or the states' Web sites for any changes that might have been enacted since you filed your last report.

Since many states have been shortening the dormancy periods to speed up unclaimed property collection (and to buffer ever-lengthening budget shortfalls), there may be some years when you will report more than one year of unclaimed property at one time. For example, Pennsylvania recently shorted their holding period for demutualized insurance company shares from seven to five years. That means that holders had to report property that would have been due over a three-report-year period all at one time. This can mean a big jump in due diligence letters, follow-up, and a larger check than would be normally reported, but would also mean fines and penalties if the holder did not know about the increased reporting requirements for the period in question. Keeping up with statutory changes will keep your policies and procedures up to date and your company out of hot water.

Record Retention Policies

One of the most important parts of any effective unclaimed property compliance program is the record retention policy. Without records to support the actions you have taken on apparently escheatable items, all of your hard work can be undone during an audit. Most of my clients have historically kept their unclaimed property records for seven years, the equivalent of the statute of limitations for a federal tax audit. Unfortunately, this is only about *half* of the time that they need to keep relevant records for an unclaimed property audit. Because the average unclaimed property audit covers ten report years, and some of the items reported for each year were created from between one and fifteen years *before the report is filed,* you can expect an auditor to request records from as far back as *25 years ago!*

What should your company's record retention policy be? While a few states, like Ohio,[1] have specific record retention policies in their unclaimed property laws, most states are silent on the issue. The states with vague record retention laws *imply,* however, that holders must keep all of the records associated with their unclaimed property and do not give any time limit.

The 1995 Uniform Act suggests that holders keep records for ten years from the time a report is filed, and most states follow this position, at least administratively. I suggest that you make this your company's policy as well. You should keep a copy of the report and *all* of the supporting data for at least ten years from the date that you file the report. This will provide you with audit protection for the periods involved and will keep your company out of the unfriendly domain of statistical sampling. Even if you are not filing reports, you should keep any and all data that you collect for unclaimed property to support your positions under audit.

Managing Your Exceptions and Exemptions

We discussed some common exceptions and exemptions from unclaimed property reporting in Chapter 5, but each department should know which exemptions and exceptions they can typically apply to the outstanding unclaimed property they are monitoring. Some common examples are:

- Business to business transactions
- Current business relationships
- Credit memos
- Gift certificate/gift cards
- Tangible personal property
- Rebates

Personnel should still keep track of these items and any backup documentation for audit support.

INTERNAL CONTROLS: CHECKS AND BALANCES

To ensure that the unclaimed property reports are being properly prepared, the individual or team who prepares the report should pass it on to another person or team for review before signing and sending the documents to the states. This is just a good business practice. Once the report is reviewed, it is ready for signatures and mailing.

The unclaimed property reports generally must be signed by a fiscally responsible corporate officer. Many states clearly list the acceptable signors. The party signing the unclaimed property report is certifying, under oath, that the report is accurate. Some reports also include the certifications that due-diligence efforts were properly performed. Because of Sarbanes-Oxley, these certifications have taken on even deeper meaning for the entities subject to their oversight. Corporate officials who sign unclaimed property reports knowing that they are false or not correct have been subjected to fines and criminal prosecution in several cases. The party who signs the report needs to meet the signatory requirements of each state's laws or bear the consequences. In most cases, these signatures will have to be notarized. Make sure that your policies and procedures manual leaves ample time between the final report preparation and the date that reports must be postmarked for final reviews and signatures to be executed. I suggest leaving a ten-day window to be safe.

INTERNAL AUDITS

If your company is large enough to have an internal audit staff, make sure that unclaimed property reviews have been added to their audit best practices schedules. If your company is smaller, you may want to assign an uninvolved employee or hire a consultant to perform a checkup on your manual and how it is being implemented on a regular basis; once every one or two years should be often enough to keep everyone on their toes!

HANDLING A DESK AUDIT OR FISHING CALL FROM A STATE AUDITOR'S OFFICE

State unclaimed property offices often call companies that they feel may not be reporting properly to ask questions about their unclaimed property policies and practices. These informal audit calls are known as *desk audits*. Incorrect or vague answers to these questions may prompt an audit investigation. To ensure that only knowledgeable and properly informed company representatives answer these questions, only specified people should give any information out about your company's unclaimed property status. When a state makes a call to anyone in your organization, your employees should not give any information to the auditor other than the name and number of the unclaimed property contact person listed in your manual. Your policies and procedures manual should name *one* person as the audit liaison or contact person for any such call to be referred to. This should typically be a person who signs the unclaimed property reports or a member of the oversight committee who can answer any inquiry swiftly and without hesitation. If the desk auditor senses weakness, they may just schedule your company for a full on-site audit.

If you include all of these matters in your policies and procedures manual and ensure that your company follows these directions, you should be prepared for *anything* that an auditor can throw at you!

NOTE

1. Ohio requires that holders keep records for five years from the time a report is filed or until an audit is completed, whichever is first (Ohio Rev Code E Ann. §169.03(F)(2)).

CHAPTER 7

Exemptions and Exceptions to Unclaimed Property Reporting

There are several exemptions and exceptions to the general rules for reporting unclaimed property to the states. Some of these exemptions are statutory and some are administrative policies, but any of these can save your company time and money if they are applied to your situation correctly. These are tricky waters, and not every exemption can be taken by every company. We will talk about the types of exemptions and how they can be integrated into your company's policies and procedures to ease your compliance burden.

There are a variety of reasons why a state might exempt a category of property from its escheat collection. The state might be attempting to appear sympathetic to businesses within its borders to tempt new businesses into its tax base, or the state might be bowing to the pressure from a lobbying group. Whatever the reason, the exemptions have to be studied separately, as most have *several* requirements that must be met to qualify for the exemption.

It is also important to remember that these exemptions are only beneficial to you, as a holder, if they apply *both in the true owner's state of last known address and in your state of incorporation.* Under the Reporting Priority Rules, as laid out by the Supreme Court in *Texas v. New Jersey,*[1] property that has an unknown address for the true owner or where the state of the owner's last known address does not collect the unclaimed property; the *holder's state of incorporation* can claim the property. This means that the property must be exempt in both states for you to be able to exclude the unclaimed property at issue from your reporting. Just keep this in mind as we discuss potential exemptions for which your company might qualify.

At this point, you have gone through your company's records to determine whether or not you have addresses for the payees of the outstanding funds and have sorted those payees into their respective states, if addresses are available, or into a list for your company's state of incorporation, if no addresses are available. Next, make sure that the property is sorted into the appropriate property type, such as payroll, accounts payable, accounts receivable, gift certificates, miscellaneous, and so forth. Each property type has a different dormancy period (the period of time that you must hold the property and attempt to find the true owner yourself before you send the money to the states). More importantly, some property types are *exempt* from unclaimed property reporting in some states!

The most common statutory exclusions from unclaimed property reporting include business-to-business transactions, gift certificates/gift cards, and tangible personal property. Because these types of property exemptions have very specific requirements, we took a closer look at what your company must consider to properly qualify your outstanding unclaimed property for the exemptions in Chapter 4, where we discussed how to determine your company's outstanding unclaimed property liability. For now, let us just say that you have done your research and you know which, if any, of the reporting exemptions that you are qualified to claim.

Business-to-Business Exemptions

In the recent past, several states have enacted legislation that exempts certain types of transactions between two businesses or commercial entities from unclaimed property reporting: the so-called business-to-business (B2B) exemption. The theory behind the B2B exemption is that businesses frequently enter into transactions with other businesses whereby the sheer volume and frequency of transactions can lead to accounting errors and over- and underpayments. These open transactions may appear to be unclaimed property, but are really just hiccups in their business dealings, which will work themselves out over the course of the business relationship. The theory continues that, as the unclaimed property laws were purportedly established to protect the rights of individuals against the unjust enrichment of the business community, rather than to clean up the financial dealings of corporations and their business associates, these savvy enterprises can be left to work out their issues with other commercial entities on their own.

To take advantage of this exemption, you must be a business dealing with another business. Many of the states have defined a business in the same way that the 1995 Uniform Property Act defined it:

> A corporation, joint stock company, investment company, partnership, unincorporated association, joint venture, limited liability company, business trust, trust company, safe deposit company, financial institution, insurance company, mutual fund, utility, or other business entity consisting of one or more persons, whether or not for profit.[2]

Although most of the baker's dozen of states that have enacted some form of the B2B exemption use the same definition of "business" as the 1995 Uniform Act, there are a few exceptions. Florida and Tennessee specifically exclude public corporations from their definition of business associations eligible to use the exemption. Massachusetts, however, specifically *includes* public corporations in the pool of businesses that can use the exemption. Illinois, Indiana, Iowa, Maryland, Massachusetts, Ohio, and Tennessee do not include *financial organizations* as parties to transactions to qualify for the B2B exemption. Before you take advantage of the B2B exemption, you need to become familiar with the quirks of each state's laws.

These transactions between two businesses have been exempted from unclaimed property reporting in thirteen states, including Arizona,[3] Florida,[4] Illinois,[5] Indiana,[6] Iowa,[7] Kansas,[8] Maryland,[9] Massachusetts,[10] North Carolina,[11] Ohio,[12] Tennessee,[13] Virginia,[14] and Wisconsin.[15] Companies that are incorporated in one of these states and transact business either (1) with other businesses within their state and/or (2) with companies in other states with the B2B exemption do not have to report any abandoned property arising from these business dealings to any unclaimed property administrator. Companies that are incorporated in a state that does *not* have a B2B exemption will find that they can gain no benefit from this exemption, no matter with whom or where they conduct business.

While the B2B exemption can provide certain holders in the applicable states with significant relief from their unclaimed property reporting burden, the exemption does not apply in all circumstances: namely, transactions conducted with individuals and transactions involving equity-related property, such as stocks and dividends. The prohibition against applying the B2B exemption to transactions involving equity-related property is clear, but the meaning of "individual" can be less certain. Property, such as an outstanding payroll or an expense check due to a former employee, will not be exempt from reporting under the B2B exemption, because the transaction involved an individual true owner. It is important to note, however, that a business that is only owned by one person, such as a single-member limited liability company or a sole proprietorship, still qualifies as a "business association" for purposes of qualifying as a holder that can take advantage of the B2B exemption. If the same expense check is made out to Tracey Reid, Esq. or to Doctor Paul Sanchez, you may still be qualified to exempt that transaction. If any of your business associates have names that, at first glance, may appear to represent individuals, you should make a note in your records that the payee of the check or the name that is assigned the credit is actually a business entity, not an individual person. This documentation will be important to save you from having the exemptions you might have taken be reversed under audit. The law is really only concerned with protecting transactions involving nonbusiness citizens.

Even states that have adopted B2B exemptions do not have blanket exemptions for every seemingly commercial transaction. Several exceptions can be found peppered throughout the statutes. For example, Wisconsin does not apply its exemption, which seems to apply only to credit balances, to transactions involving any bank or financial institution. As with any exemption, the law is construed narrowly in favor of the state, rather than the citizen, so be cautious when creating policies in your company to take advantage of B2B exemptions. As there are only a few states that provide this potential exemption, we will discuss the state specifics:

- *Arizona* exempts (1) accounts payable balances of business associations of $50 or less payable to another business association and (2) property of a person who is maintaining a current business relationship with the holder.
- *Florida* exempts property that is issued or shown as owed to another entity by a business that is subject to the jurisdiction of the United States Surface Transportation Board or its successor federal agency if the owner has no such obligation to pay that to the department.
- *Illinois* exempts B2B transactions in the normal and ordinary course of business.

- *Indiana* exempts B2B credit memoranda or credit balances resulting from those memoranda. It also exempts transactions between business entities and a "motor carrier," which is defined to include any business characterized as a common carrier, motor carrier, water carrier, freight forwarder, contract carrier, or carrier certified in accordance with rules adopted by both the Indiana legislature and the federal government.[16]
- *Iowa* exempts credit memoranda shown on the books and records of a business association with respect to another business association, unless the balance is held by a banking organization or financial organization.
- *Kansas* exempts any outstanding check, draft, credit balance, customer overpayment, or unidentified remittance issued to a business association as part of a commercial transaction in the ordinary course of a holder's business.
- *Maryland* exempts outstanding checks or credits issued to vendors or commercial customers in the ordinary course of a holder's business, unless that property is held by a bank or financial institution.
- *Massachusetts* exempts property arising out of a transaction occurring in the normal and ordinary course of business.
- *North Carolina* exempts credit balances shown on the records of a business association to or for the benefit of another business association.
- *Ohio* exempts any payment or credit due to a business association from a business association rendered in the course of business, as well as tangible goods sold or services performed in the course of business.
- *Tennessee* exempts transactions in the ordinary course of a holder's business when the entities have an *ongoing business relationship*. Tennessee defines an ongoing relationship as one in which the holder has engaged in a transaction with the business or a predecessor-in-interest after the date of the outstanding check, draft, and so on.
- *Virginia* exempts credit balances and outstanding checks resulting from or attributable to the sale of goods or services to a business association.
- *Wisconsin* exempts credit balances issued to a commercial customer account by a business association in the ordinary course of business, unless the credit balance is property held by a banking organization or financial organization.

What can you take away from all of these exceptions? It is important that you read the fine print in the laws granting these exemptions. While dealings with financial institutions and banks seem to be the most limited business transactions, it is important to note that the laws in several states required transactions to be *in the ordinary course of business* for the holder to be able to exempt them from unclaimed property reporting. We discussed ordinary course of business in Chapter 2 when discussing whether something was technically reportable as unclaimed property. If you are a manufacturer, transactions in your ordinary course of business are going to be different from ordinary transactions for a retailer or restaurant. In some state laws, it is also required that the two business associations have an ongoing business relationship for the holder to take advantage of the exemption. We are going to discuss what ongoing business relationship means in the next section, but it bears mentioning that a one-time transaction, even with an otherwise qualified business, will not meet the requirements of the exemption in some states. As with any statutory exemptions, you need to narrowly construe the law and apply it with caution to your situation. Sometimes, just reporting the property is less work than proving it is exempt!

CURRENT BUSINESS RELATIONSHIP

This is also known as an *ongoing business relationship*. As mentioned in the previous discussion about the B2B relationship, one of the elements necessary to claim the B2B exemption in some states is that your business and the other entity that you are holding the check or credit for be in a *current business relationship*. What is a current business relationship? Most statutes, even the ones that require it, do not bother to define it. The state of Texas, which does not have a formal exemption for B2B transactions, tells holders in the instructions for its unclaimed property report that "balances owed to current customers should not be reported."[17] Texas does not have case law OR administrative law to help out in this area!

In most cases, whether this current or ongoing relationship exists is a subjective decision. It is very rarely spelled out in statute. One of the rare exceptions is the state of Tennessee. In Tennessee, a current business relationship is defined in their statute as one where you had at least one business transaction with the business or its predecessor-in-interest after the date of the outstanding items according to your books and records. This seems to mean that even having one single completed transaction dated after the date of your outstanding transaction with that Tennessee business is enough to keep any of your outstanding checks or credits from being reportable unclaimed property in that state.

Most other states, however, are silent on the issue. If you were to call the state of Maryland, for example, a state which requires a current business relationship to claim their B2B exemption, you might get the same response that I got, which was that if you do not have a current business relationship, you cannot claim the credit; incredibly helpful, isn't it? Some other states, like Indiana and Wisconsin, have no formal rule on the meaning of current vendors, with exemptions considered on a case-by-case basis. During a recent audit conducted by the state of California, the auditor in charge of my client's examination agreed that a current business relationship would be any completed transaction within three years after the date of the dormant or unclaimed transaction. This is certainly a vast difference from the ruling that I got from Arizona, stating that their policy for determining the existence of a current business relationship was that there must have been a completed transaction with the other business within the last year.

This lack of guidance in either the statutory or administrative law of most states makes it difficult to judge whether or not you can claim this statutory exemption for businesses with whom you are less active. I have two different approaches. If I am dealing with an audit situation, my rule of thumb is that if the state has a conditional B2B statutory exemption, unless I have advice from the state giving me a different time period, I only attempt to make the statutorily exempted B2B claim if my client had transacted business with the other enterprise within one year from the date of the unclaimed transaction. If I am operating under current compliance circumstances, I am a little more aggressive and use a three-year transaction rule. If my client has transacted business within the last three years, then we can take the B2B exemption. Of course, if I have received guidance from one of the states on this issue, I follow their suggested time frames.

The current business relationship defense to reporting unclaimed transactions is not necessarily limited to the states where the B2B exemption exists. It can be claimed informally in states where there is no statutory exception for outstanding credits or checks to business payees. While it is not widely publicized, most states will allow holders to claim the current business relationship defense to remitting outstanding unclaimed property during an audit or a voluntary disclosure review. You can liken it to performing informal due diligence to remove outstanding transactions from your list of reportable property when you are *currently* (meaning in the last 12 months) conducting business with an entity that has an outstanding credit or check sitting on your records. This will only work for transactions due to other businesses, not for items that are outstanding and due to individuals. In the past, many companies would attempt, for example, to remove outstanding payroll checks and expense reimbursement checks from their reportable escheat property lists if they were due to current employees. The states are not accepting of this defense and still require a due diligence letter signed by the current employee stating that nothing is due and owing to them before they will allow a company to delete the outstanding checks from their reportable property lists. They are more lenient with business transactions and I would encourage you to consider the possibility for your own current business relationships.

GIFT CERTIFICATES/GIFT CARDS

When compared to the age of most types of property traditionally subject to abandoned property laws, gift certificates and gift cards are the new kids on the block. The paper gift certificates that first appeared in the 1980s were replaced by the new product, electronic gift cards, introduced to the world in the late 1990s by Blockbuster and Neiman-Marcus. The newest metamorphosis has been to the reloadable electronic gift cards, or stored value cards, that can have value added over and over again. Some online retailers, such as bn.com, are now selling electronic gift certificates that are only redeemable for online purchases and cannot be used in a brick and mortar store. These retail phenomena are some of the most strongly lobbied exemptions in the unclaimed property arena.

In the unclaimed property world, most states consider gift certificates and gift cards to be intangible personal property subject to unclaimed property reporting. Some state laws are not clear about what they consider gift cards to be, either tangible or intangible, but by administrative practice, collect them under their catch-all unclaimed property laws. Still other states either specifically exempt unredeemed gift cards from their definition of escheatable property or have specifically removed these retail power-players from their definitions of reportable property types to exclude them from collection. The most recent legislation surrounding gift cards and gift certificates in most states is actually happening in the consumer protection arena, where laws are being put into place to protect consumers from losing their ability to use old gift certificates and gift cards, therefore removing them from escheatment by default. While an entire book could probably be written on the subject of gift-certificate unclaimed property law, we will just touch on the highlights in this chapter. If you are a business dealing with gift certificates and electronic gift cards, or the even-newer genre of electronic gift certificates and reloadable stored value cards, it is important to know where you stand with the states in which you may be subject to unclaimed property reporting, as well as to be aware of the planning opportunities available that can help ease your unclaimed property burden for these retail megasellers.

The retail industry overall sold $35 billion in gift cards during the 2007 Christmas season alone. Of that $35 billion, 10%, or a staggering $3.5 billion, will go unredeemed.[18] This is known in the retail industry as "breakage." Since retailers make an average 40% profit on the sale of merchandise, they lose 100% of their profit if they have to escheat the full face value of their gift cards that go unredeemed and they do not recoup the cost of administering a gift card program. Since their inception, issuers have attempted to limit their losses for unredeemed gift certificates and gift cards. Retailers started with expiration dates. They would give the gift certificate recipient a limited period of time, usually between six months and one year, to redeem the certificate or it would expire and the retailer did not have to honor the value for a purchase. Mistakenly, most of these retailers traditionally believed that allowing the gift certificate to expire was enough of a "contract" term between themselves and the purchaser or recipient to keep the proceeds from the gift card from being reportable unclaimed property. They were incorrect. While the legal trend seems to be to exempt gift cards from unclaimed property collection, most states require certain criteria to be met to keep those cards from escheating. Because consumer advocacy groups have lobbied so diligently, most states are setting *minimum* periods within which a gift card must be redeemable (usually one or two years) or are requiring that gift cards sold in their states have no expiration date or retailers must escheat the full face value of the gift cards.

The area of unclaimed property law dealing with gift certificates and their progeny is developing rapidly. At least 33 states have passed laws giving either a complete or partial exemption from reporting gift certificates, although almost all of them carry a list of criteria that must be met to use the exemption. The states basically fall into five groups where gift certificates are concerned:

1. *The "gift certificates are not escheatable property" group.* This group includes Arizona, Connecticut, Indiana, Maryland, Minnesota, and Virginia. The laws in these states simply exempt gift cards from the list of property that is escheatable to their state. They do not audit for them, and they do not collect unredeemed gift cards or their proceeds from retailers. These are the states where retailers can put the GiftCo planning we will discuss later in the chapter to good use.

2. *The "no expiration or you must escheat" group.* This group includes states like California, North Carolina, Texas, Washington, and Massachusetts. These states do not collect unredeemed gift cards from retailers as long as the gift cards do not have an expiration date, and retailers must agree to redeem the gift cards at their full face value (or the amount remaining on a partially redeemed card) for eternity.

3. *The "60/40" states.* This group includes states like Indiana and Iowa that allow retailers to put expiration dates on gift cards sold in their states, but make retailers report 60% of the face value of the unredeemed gift certificates as unclaimed property when the dormancy period is up. These states allow the retailers to keep the 40% that would have represented the markup they would profit from if the gift cards had been redeemed for merchandise.

4. *The "gift cards cannot expire but you must still escheat" group.* This group is the most confusing and includes the state of Connecticut. The law generally requires that gift cards sold in these states contain no expiration date, but they must still be escheated to the state at the end of the dormancy period, which begins running on the date that the gift card is sold. Retailers are required to honor gift cards in these states, no matter how old they are, and if the funds have already been escheated to the state, the retailer can apply for a refund from the unclaimed property administrator.

5. *The "exempt by omission" group.* This group includes Florida, Kansas, New Jersey, North Dakota, Oregon, South Carolina, and Wisconsin. In these states, gift cards have been removed from the state laws describing reportable unclaimed property. As there is no reference to gift certificates and gift cards in the law, holders do not have to report them to these "silent" states.

We have included a chart in Appendix F that summarizes the current gift certificate laws by state. As always, you should discuss any potential legal issues with your corporate counsel or outside legal representative. These laws are changing fast; try to keep up!

It is also important to note that not all states have updated their laws to reflect the changing gift certificate forms. Most state laws do not yet address gift cards, reloadable gift cards, or electronic gift certificates. While the states will assuredly catch up with the new terminology eventually, you should be careful to examine the unclaimed property laws in all of the states to determine what form of gift is or is not covered by any potential exemptions. It is my opinion that, where not expressly addressed by a state's statute, the unclaimed property division will treat unclaimed gift cards and electronic gift certificates in the same way that it treated paper gift certificates in the past.

It is also unclear in the law of most states whether reloading a gift card resets the clock for dormancy or whether the dormancy clock is still set from the date of the original purchase. As the law develops in this area, significant statutory changes will have to be made to accommodate the changing technology. As the law stands now, it is unclear in most states whether the reloading of the gift card will be considered activity that tolls the dormancy period from running. The issue has been addressed in a handful of states, including Texas and Maine. The consensus with these few states is that gift cards are determined to be abandoned on the later of the following two options: (1) the expiration of the dormancy period from the time of purchase, if the card has not been used; or (2) the expiration of the dormancy period from the date that the card was last reloaded with value. It will probably follow in the rest of the states that reloading a stored value card will reset the dormancy clock for reporting purposes, but there is no telling how long these statutory adjustments might take. If you are concerned with this issue, remember that you can always request an opinion letter from any state administrators who might govern your company's activities. You can rely on this opinion under audit and prevent penalties and interest from being applied if the tide of change does not go in your favor!

If you are a relatively small business that only sells a few gift certificates or gift cards each year, you are probably just interested in knowing how the law in your state or states treats gift cards. There are states that have a 100% unconditional gift certificate exemption: Arizona, Connecticut, Indiana, Maryland, Minnesota, and Virginia. These states do not audit for and will not accept unclaimed gift cards. While this is also interesting to those of you considering a GiftCo, it is also nice to know that you do not have to track your unredeemed gift card sales for these states. Consumer protection groups, intent on protecting the rights of consumers to keep the value of their gift cards until they choose to use them, have influenced the development of guidelines in several states to keep gift cards from expiring, as well as avoiding escheat. Some states have very specific limitations on the way that a company administers its gift card program in order for the gift cards to be exempt from escheat, however. In Delaware, for example, holders are not required to report unredeemed gift certificates that are valued at $5 or less and are issued by certain food-service issuers.[19] The states having a *partial* exemption for gift certificates and gift cards are Colorado, Nebraska, New Hampshire, Utah, and Wyoming.

Other states exempt all gift cards sold by certain types of businesses. For example, Alabama appears to only exempt gift cards, gift certificates, or in-store merchandise credits that are issued by persons or businesses that are primarily in the business of selling tangible personal property at retail.[20] This means that places like day spas that primarily sell *services* would still need to escheat their unredeemed gift certificates. Still more jurisdictions have a 100% conditional gift certificate and gift card exemption, including Alabama, Arkansas, California, Idaho, Illinois, Massachusetts, North Carolina, Ohio, Rhode Island, Tennessee, and Washington. Then there are the states that offer a *partial, conditional* exemption for gift certificates and gift cards: Delaware, Maine, Missouri, Montana, New Mexico, and West Virginia. While the statutes in these states vary, most require that some conditions be met to make gift certificates and gift cards exempt from unclaimed property reporting. Generally, the gift certificates/cards need to have *no expiration date* to be exempt from unclaimed property reporting. Check with each state for its specific requirements. I have included gift card/gift certificate exemption information in Appendix F.

GIFT CARD CORPORATIONS

The gift certificate breakage area can be costly to retailers. If they are incorporated in a state that does not exempt gift cards and they do not collect name and address information for all of the gift cards that they sell, under *Texas v. New Jersey*[21] they have to remit the entire face value of all unredeemed gift cards to their state of incorporation. Many retailers are now taking advantage of planning that can potentially remove *all* of your company's gift certificate or gift card sales from your escheatable property list. The GiftCo has been developed to put all of your gift cards out of the reach of states that grasp for the large amount of gift card funds that go unclaimed every year. To avoid having to turn their profits over to the states, many companies opt to incorporate a separate gift card subsidiary in a state that does not required escheatment of unredeemed gift cards. A state like Virginia, which does not collect unredeemed gift card balances, is a likely choice for the incorporation of one of these entities.

The typical plan for GiftCo savings is to form a new company to assume all of your gift card operations in a state with a 100% exemption for the sale of gift certificates and gift cards, such as Arizona, Connecticut, Indiana, Maryland, Minnesota, or Virginia.[22] You would then shift all of your gift card activity into the GiftCo. The GiftCo is given all operations related to gift certificates, including issuing the cards, registering them, and tracking card balances. It is important that the terms of the gift cards being issued meet all of the requirements for exemption from unclaimed property reporting in the state where you are organizing the GiftCo. To ensure that the new entity is not considered a "shell" by the unclaimed property and taxing authorities, it is important that this new company operate as any legitimate company would, with bank accounts, employees, boards of directors, its own letterhead, and so on.

The theory behind the GiftCo is relatively straightforward: The GiftCo provides gift cards to you, the retailer. While the retailer is selling the cards to purchasers, the GiftCo is still the company obligated to guarantee the amount of value on the gift card. The retailer merely sells the gift cards on behalf of the GiftCo for a commission or percentage of the face value of the gift card. The retailer remits the proceeds of the gift card sale to GiftCo (minus their commission, of course). When the end-user redeems his or her gift card at a retail location, the retailer fulfills the sale with merchandise but presents the total sale to the GiftCo for reimbursement, and the GiftCo sends money back to the retailer (minus their transaction fee, of course). All of these savings are contingent, however, on the fact that no name and address information is collected by the retailer when these gift certificates are sold. If you routinely collect name and address information because, in the normal course of your business, you personalize or mail gift cards to individuals, then *Texas v. New Jersey*[23] would apply. The law would dictate that any unclaimed gift cards would be remitted (1) to the state of the owner's last known address (if they collected unclaimed gift cards) and (2) to your GiftCo's state of incorporation, where they would be exempt.

If your company does not want the hassle of operating an entirely separate legal entity, you can outsource your gift card function to a third-party service provider that will act as a GiftCo for your company and assume the legal responsibility for any unclaimed property reporting that may crop up, freeing you to enjoy your profits.

There are a few considerations to take into account before creating a GiftCo, however. You need to get your legal department or outside counsel involved in the discussion. You need to consider the legal form of a GiftCo, whether you want to expose your entity to a new legal domicile, the cost of forming a separate legal entity, how moving the GiftCo operations will impact your business, how you will structure any intercompany transactions and intercompany pricing, and the ever-present federal and state tax implications of forming a whole new entity. There may be regulatory issues, new unclaimed property reporting obligations, and many other concerns to weigh. If, all things considered, you still find that the benefits outweigh the detriments, your legal counsel should be able to create an entity that will allow you to keep your gift card breakage all to yourself!

DORMANCY FEES

Retailers have also tried to recoup some of the value of their outstanding and unredeemed gift certificates and gift cards by tacking on *administrative fees* or *dormancy fees* that reduce the amount of the gift certificate or gift card by a fixed percent or increment every month that it went unredeemed, until the value was reduced to nothing. Retailers argue that the cost of manufacturing, tracking, and redeeming gift card programs is costly, so the fees are not unreasonable. Needless to say, this was not very popular with consumer advocacy groups. Pressure from their constituencies has forced most states to ban these types of administrative or dormancy fees for gift cards unless *very strict* criteria are met. The legal treatment of unclaimed property service charges and dormancy fees are not always limited to the unclaimed property laws in each state. Consumer protection laws, banking regulations, and other federal and state statutory provisions can affect these charges, and you should have your legal advisor thoroughly review the entire body of law in this area for each state involved before you begin imposing any of these types of fees.

The treatments of service charges and dormancy fees have split the states into three distinct groups:

1. *Service charges are prohibited under the Unclaimed Property Laws.* For example, the state of Texas prohibits dormancy fees or service charges on most types of intangible property.[24]
2. *Service charges are permitted under the Unclaimed Property Laws.* States with this type of law allow holders to deduct the value of the service charges from the amount of money remitted to the state as unclaimed property.
3. *Service charges are addressed under the Consumer Protection Laws.* States that address service fees in their consumer protection laws generally prohibit these types of fees, except in a few cases, where the certificates are issued as a charitable contribution, an award, or a loyalty program reward.[25]

In states that allow dormancy fees and service charges to be applied to unclaimed property, there are generally criteria that must be met for the charges to be considered legitimate. The 1995 Uniform Unclaimed Property Act gives a list of requirements that are the basis for most state laws in this area. The 1995 act requires that any service charges or dormancy fees meet three requirements to be considered legitimate:

1. An enforceable contract must exist between the holder and the owner to establish the holder's right to impose the charge.

2. The holder must, in fact, regularly and consistently apply the charge without regularly refunding the charge if an owner claims the abandoned property.

3. The amount of the charge must be reasonable, based on the facts and circumstance of the transactions.

While some states, like Ohio, permit holders to deduct a small fee from the value of each unclaimed item remitted to cover their administrative costs, most states frown upon any attempt that holders make to reduce the value of abandoned property for their own gain. Most holders would be wise to avoid charging these types of service charges at all, but if you feel that you can legitimately meet the requirements, remember that they must be *strictly enforced.* Your policy to apply service charges or dormancy fees must be clearly spelled out to the purchaser, in writing, somewhere conspicuous. Just putting notice of these charges in fine print somewhere in the transaction documents will most likely be disallowed as notice by unclaimed property enforcement agencies. You also have to be very consistent in both applying and not removing these service charges. If you regularly reinstate the service charges for people that complain, or good customers that come back after a period of being absent, you will fail to prove your case to an unclaimed property administrator and the dormancy fees that you did not reimburse will be reinstated on your unclaimed property audit assessment.

You will also need to be reasonable about the rate and amount of any service charges that you impose. If the dollar or two a month that you charge after a gift certificate or savings account has been abandoned for the statutory dormancy period is reasonable and is applied to cover the cost of tracking the true owner, performing due diligence, and paying for postage, most administrators would probably allow the deductions. If, however, the amount of the charges is unreasonable, such as $1 a day after the property reaches dormancy, and it appears that the sole purpose of the charges is to reduce the value of the outstanding unclaimed property to zero and avoid escheat, an administrator will probably disallow ALL of your dormancy charges. Service charges are tricky. These dormancy fees should carry a warning: "Proceed with Caution."

Customer Credits/Credit Balances

Here is an area that continually confuses holders. There is more than one way to attempt to stop an unclaimed property auditor from taking your customer credits or other credit balances, but some states have helped holders out by exempting credit balances statutorily. These exemptions may be total or partial, and even industry-specific or credit type–specific, but you will need to check the laws of each state to find your potential savings. Some states, such as Virginia, offer 100% unconditional credit balance exemptions. Other states, including Arizona, Colorado, Florida, and Idaho, offer partial exemptions. Oklahoma and Wyoming only exempt credit memos. Alabama and Arkansas offer an exemption *only* for in-store merchandise credits. Missouri exempts *part* of your credit balances in that they only require holders to report 60% of the value and only report those credit balances that are redeemable only for merchandise. This area is rife with exceptions and limitations, so read the fine print of each state's law carefully before making it your company's policy to exempt all customer credits from unclaimed property reporting.

Tangible Personal Property

While most of what we have been discussing in this unclaimed property arena has centered on intangibles, some holders, depending on their line of business, may find themselves in possession of tangible personal property on occasion. Perhaps you are a casino or a restaurant with a coat check. Maybe you are a hotel with room safes. Most commonly, you might be a bank with safe-deposit boxes. Almost every business has a Lost and Found. You are probably wondering if you have to report unclaimed tangible property like you do the intangible types. The answer is, "Maybe." The truth of the matter is that tangible personal property, in the unclaimed property law, is basically separated into two categories: (1) safe-deposit box contents and (2) everything else.

Entire books can and have been written about the property laws surrounding lost, abandoned, and mislaid real and tangible personal property. Without delving into that arena, as it is beyond the scope of this book, I will just tell you that most unclaimed property administrators do not want anything sent to them except money; they just do not have the room to store the contents of someone's Lost and Found box. Unless something has a fair market value worth more than the cost to the administrator of advertising or storing it (such as diamond jewelry or collectibles), most holders are not required to send tangible personal property to any state with their reports. State laws will differ, but each state clearly states its policy regarding tangible personal property in its unclaimed or abandoned property reports. Check the instructions for the states where you have a physical presence to find out if there are any minimum values for reporting tangible personal property or if you are supposed to attempt to sell the items and remit the value with your unclaimed property report. This will most likely be a very rare event.

That being said, the states generally do want things with intrinsic market value. They simply sell them and deposit the proceeds into an account under the name of the apparent true owner. This leads to our discussion about the exception to this general rule regarding exemptions for tangible personal property, which surrounds the administration of safe-deposit boxes.

As anyone in the banking industry can attest, the abandoned contents of safe-deposit boxes are considered reportable unclaimed property in almost all, if not every, jurisdiction of the United States. While the dormancy periods for this type of property are generally long, averaging five years, once the boxes are determined to be abandoned, the holder (in most cases, the bank) is required to open the boxes, take inventory of the contents and either (1) send the contents in their entirety to the state unclaimed property administrator, (2) assess the value of the contents and send only items with intrinsic value to the administrator, or (3) sell the valuable items in the open market and send the proceeds to the state unclaimed property administrator.

Banks are not the only businesses that may have tangible personal property that is escheatable under the same law that governs safe-deposit boxes. The 1995 Uniform Act defined property subject to escheat to include:

> . . . tangible personal property described in Section 3 or a fixed and certain interest in intangible personal property that is held, issued or owed in the course of a holder's business, or by a government, governmental subdivision, agency, or instrumentality, and all income or increments there from.[26]

Some private companies, like jewelers and furriers, maintain storage lockers and storage services for their clients. These types of safe storage facilities and their valuable contents might also be subject to the unclaimed property laws surrounding safe-deposit boxes. Public storage businesses are constantly being left with lockers full of unclaimed tangible property and customers who have stopped paying their bills. If your company offers these types of services, make sure that you check the applicable laws in the states where your storage facilities are located. You may be obligated, under the law, to escheat the valuable property or the proceeds from its sale.

NOTES

1. *Texas v. New Jersey*, 379 U.S. 674 (1965).
2. 1995 Uniform Unclaimed Property Act §1(3).
3. Ariz. Rev. Stat. Ann. §44-301-15.
4. §717.117(1)(H), Fla. Stat. (2007).
5. 765 Ill. Rev. Stat. §1025/2a.
6. Ind. Code Ann. §32-34-1-1(c).
7. Iowa Code Ann. §556.1(9).
8. Kan. Stat. Ann. §58-3935(g).
9. Md. Comm. Code §17-101(m).
10. Mass Gen. Laws Ann., Chapter 200A, §5.
11. N.C. Gen. Stat. §116-54(e).
12. Ohio Rev. Code Ann. §169.01(B)(2)(b).
13. Tenn. Code Ann. §66-29-104(3).
14. Va. Code Ann. §55-210.8:1.
15. Wisc. Stat. Ann. §177.01(10)(B).
16. Ind. Code Ann. §32-34-1-17(c)(1)-(2).
17. Texas Unclaimed Property Reporting Instructions 2007, p. 15.
18. James Covert, "Serious Money." *The New York Post Online*, Dec. 30, 2007 (www.nypost.com/seven/12302007/business/serious_money_384584.htm)
19. See *12 Del. C. Sec. 1199(g)* (2004); 30 DEL. C. Sec. 2906 (2004).
20. Ala. Code Sec. 35-12-24.1 (2004).
21. *Texas v. New Jersey*, 379 U.S. 674 (1965).
22. If you already have a GiftCo subsidiary, you can also just reorganize in one of these retailer-friendly states.
23. *Texas v. New Jersey*, 379 U.S. 674 (1965).
24. Effective September 1, 2005, except with respect to service charges on money orders or stored value cards, Texas law specifically prohibits service charges on abandoned property. Tex. Peop. Code §72.103.
25. For example, Haw. Rev. Stat. §481B-13(c).
26. Uniform Unclaimed Property Act (NCCUSL 1995) §1(13).

CHAPTER 8

Special Industry Considerations

Almost every business entity is subject to the unclaimed property laws of at least one state, if not multiple states. Some industries are subject to more than just the general rules, though. While we cannot cover every special circumstance for every type of business, we are going to discuss some of the most obvious unique issues for a few businesses that have more than their fair share of attention from unclaimed property administrators and their audit staffs.

INSURANCE

The insurance industry is one of the most audited business enterprises in the unclaimed property universe. As they deal with so many types of potentially unclaimed property, the states have kept a watch on insurance companies for quite a while now. The insurance industry is so scrutinized under the unclaimed property laws that they even have separate filing dates for their reports in some cases! Different types of insurance will also have different treatments under the unclaimed property laws. While most states have a November 1 filing deadline for unclaimed property compliance, the reports of insurance companies, especially life insurance companies, are bound to have a different filing date. For example, while life insurance companies in Arizona, Arkansas, California, Colorado, Delaware, and the District of Columbia all have May 1 compliance deadlines, all other businesses report on November 1. In Connecticut, all reports are due on March 31. In Kentucky, all reports are due on November 1. In Maryland, life insurance companies must report by April 30. If you are in the life insurance industry, or if a portion of your business sells life insurance, you may have five or more potential reporting deadlines each year! That is certainly enough to keep your unclaimed property department on their toes.

Offers to Settle

Several property types specific to the insurance industries have been problematic for holders for some time. The first is *insurance drafts and checks*. Under audit, many insurance companies find themselves fighting huge assessments listing thousands of uncashed settlement checks. If your accounting systems do not distinguish between outstanding offers in settlement that are issued but never cashed and liquidated obligations that are outstanding but subject to open cases or litigation, you will also find yourself with an unusually long list of potentially damaging unclaimed property. Unclaimed property law distinguishes between (1) unaccepted offers of settlement (which are not considered unclaimed property) and (2) unpresented drafts or checks representing liquidated obligations (which can be presumed abandoned and will be reportable unclaimed property).

The case law in this area has most often dealt with the property and casualty insurance industry. Unfortunately, the courts have been divided in their opinions. Some cases have held that the state cannot collect offers in settlement as unclaimed property if they cannot prove that the obligation has been settled and is no longer subject to litigation.[1] Other courts have ruled that holders should file reports including all outstanding drafts and offers in settlement, and show why the presumption of abandonment is incorrect.[2]

In the life, health, and disability insurance arena, courts have almost always ruled that checks or drafts issued for these types of insurance are not offers to settle. The leading cases have held that these types of checks are actually unclaimed property, because they are in payment of fixed or scheduled benefits, owing in the ordinary course of the insurer's business, and thus are reportable after the dormancy period expires. In short, checks are not issued by insurance companies unless a proper bill for services already rendered has been presented to them for payment on behalf of someone that they are contractually obligated to pay for. As these types of payments are not usually in dispute, they are escheatable if not settled before the dormancy period runs.

What can an insurance company do to make sure that they are not paying inflated amounts of unclaimed property over to the states? They need to keep good records, distinguishing whether the checks are offers in settlement or fixed payment drafts, to defend their positions. If you are still unsure how to treat outstanding claims drafts, there are a few general rules you can apply.

In the health/life/disability area, the claimant's right under the insurance contract to the claim check or draft is usually more definite and fixed, based on the occurrence of a certain event such as a death, illness, or disability. In these cases, the obligation is liquidated and will likely be considered unclaimed property by the states.

In the third-party casualty/property area, the contract right of the policy holder or claimant may not be fixed and will often be contingent on establishing some sort of liability for damages. In these cases where the right to payment is not so firmly established, the claims checks or drafts are probably offers to settle, and will not be considered sufficiently liquidated to be reportable as unclaimed property. The outcome may be different, however, if liability has been established either by an agreement among the parties or by a court of law and the claim payment check remains outstanding. In this case, unless the established debt has been settled in another way, the outstanding check will be considered liquidated damages and will be subject to unclaimed property reporting once the appropriate dormancy period has passed.

There is also some distinction made between first-party drafts and third-party drafts. First-party drafts are checks written to cover policy obligations, such as paying an insured's medical expenses or car repair bill when an accident occurs. Since these types of checks are, in practice, not usually issued unless a claim or proof of loss has been submitted, they are considered to be more fixed, thus qualifying as unclaimed property. Third-party drafts, however, are usually issued as an offer to settle in cases where the contract right is contingent on establishing liability, such as in a car accident in which both parties were cited for a moving violation by the authorities and there is some doubt as to which driver actually caused an accident or which driver is more at fault. These types of checks, since the liability is in question, do not usually represent liquidated damages and will not be unclaimed property.

Whether or not a check is a reportable fixed payment or an exempt offer to settle is often a fact-specific decision and will depend on the terms of the individual underlying insurance policy. In general, it has been held that states have the burden of proving that something is escheatable,[3] but this burden may sometimes shift to the holder if the property that the state is attempting to collect is typically escheatable property.[4] Wherever the burden of proof lies, you, as the holder, will have to be able to point to language in the policy and how this language is administered to defend your position that certain checks are not unclaimed property. To do that, you need to *maintain good records*! Keep the claims files available and reference the appropriate claims file on your checks. If you do not already do so, you can print release information on the check itself, as well as the maximum period of time that an offer of settlement check is valid for presentation to your company as a valid settlement acceptance. You can be sure that the auditors will review these items closely if you are chosen for an audit.

Demutualization of Shares

In the past few years, many insurance companies have gone through demutualization, meaning that they were previously owned by policy-holders but have been converted to shareholder ownership. After demu-tualization, policyholders are all issued shares of the new company's stock, and they maintain their insurance coverage according to their original policy terms. Since many of these insurance companies' policyholders held policies that had been paid in full for some time, their names and addresses were often lost; as a result, many of these new shareholders were not easy to locate. Some policyholders had moved or died between the time of paying their policies in full and the date of the demutualization. Historically, states used the general dormancy period applicable to prop-erty held by insurance companies for collection of abandoned shares of demutualized insurance companies. In the past few years, however, several states have created a special category of unclaimed property for abandoned demutualized shares and have given them a much shorter dormancy period to speed up their collection by the states. The typical holding period for demutualized shares is now two to five years (down from the original average of seven to ten years) from the date of demutualization, unless the owner of the newly issued shares has communicated in some way with the holder. If your company has gone through this type of transi-tion, you should have adjusted your policies and procedures to reflect the more limited holding periods you have for abandoned demutualized shares. You would have also been required to lump together several years of due diligence efforts and report unclaimed funds to cover all of the years that disappeared from your dormancy periods, as well as the property that was reportable for your current year when these dormancy reduction laws went into effect. This approach has allowed states to line their coffers with a plethora of unclaimed money over the past few years. If your company did not adjust its reporting to reflect these shorter dormancy periods, you should consider a voluntary disclosure agreement (VDA) with any states that you are late in paying. It will save you penalties, if not interest, when the unclaimed property auditors come calling!

Banking

The banking industry was one of the first big targets that reinvigorated unclaimed property administrators set their sights on in the 1980s. In fact, in some jurisdictions, banking and financial institutions were the only types of businesses that were audited for many years. Perhaps this was because their entire industry deals with nothing but potentially unclaimed property: savings accounts, checking accounts, certificates of deposit, safe-deposit boxes, individual retirement accounts, and so forth. While the audit lottery has shifted its focus to other industries in recent years, banks have had renewed scrutiny lately with both the Banker's Trust[5] case and all of the class action lawsuits in California over wrongfully escheated safe-deposit box contents and bank accounts. As we have already discussed, the banking industry is almost completely excluded from taking advantage of any business-to-business (B2B) exemptions. Several more unclaimed property issues specific to the banking industry are causing a few sticking points with holders and states trying to keep these institutions in compliance.

When Is an Account Considered Dormant?

The banking industry faces one major issue that has not yet been resolved by most state laws or administrative policies: the effect of electronic transactions, such as balance enquiries at automated teller machines, on the dormancy status of otherwise abandoned accounts. While the laws are not consistent across the states, as Web-banking and automatic deposits and withdrawals become more common than teller-to-customer contact, these are going to have to be addressed. The common theme among the states that I have informally canvassed seems to be that electronic enquiries that require a personal identification number (PIN) or other secret identification information to be entered will probably be considered enough activity to keep an account from becoming dormant. Since the very nature of these PINs makes them unique to each customer, and they are generally kept private, it is believed that only the customer would be using them to make an account enquiry, so these enquiries might, therefore, be deemed customer contact. For a business to rely on this type of transaction, though, the bank would have to keep records of these transactions and have some way to track the use of the PINs and secret identification information.

What Fees Can Be Imposed on Dormant Accounts?

The unclaimed property world has actually been quite lenient on banks' imposition of service charges on dormant accounts. In most states, as long as the customer is made aware of the potential for these charges when the account is opened, or in writing when the policies change, the banks have gotten away with reducing accounts with little to no activity down to zero and, therefore, avoiding escheating of these funds. While the law is a bit lackadaisical, it is important to be aware that the federal Truth-in-Savings Act may impose some restrictions on the imposition of these fees. You should definitely have your legal counsel review the appropriate law in this area.

Safe-Deposit Boxes

In recent months, the disposition of abandoned safe-deposit boxes has become a real hot point in the media. While the states require financial institutions to drill the abandoned safe-deposit boxes and turn the contents over to them for safekeeping, the state sometimes allows the banks to pick and choose what has commercial value and to use their discretion to dispose of worthless items. I would caution you that this discretion can get you into worlds of trouble if, for example, you drill the contents of an especially sentimental family, decide the family photos and mementos are without commercial value on the open market, and dispose of the items without sending them to the state. You will undoubtedly get your bank's name splashed all over the press. I would suggest that you send the *entire* contents of all safe-deposit boxes to the appropriate states and let *them* take the heat for destroying sacred family mementos. You do not need that kind of negative publicity! Also, make sure that you search your records thoroughly for *any* other customer activity in other accounts before you drill a safe-deposit box and destroy or transfer the contents. Current customers will certainly *not* appreciate what happens to the valuables that they thought were entrusted safely in your hands, especially if they have an active mortgage or checking account with one of your branch offices!

Money Orders and Traveler's Checks

Here are two property types, typically sold by financial institutions, that do not follow the escheat jurisdictional rules of *Texas v. New Jersey*. The federal government passed legislation in 1976 to specifically lay out the priority for the escheatment of abandoned money orders and traveler's checks. Under the Disposition of Abandoned Money Orders and Traveler's Checks Act,[6] a state can claim abandoned money orders and traveler's checks if it is either (1) the state where the money order or traveler's check was purchased, or (2) the state in which the issuer's principal place of business is located. This is an important exception to the normal priority rules and should be dealt with in your institution's policy and procedure manual.

Health Care

Whether your company is a hospital, doctor's group, nursing home, or rehabilitation center, the most common unclaimed property types that you will probably deal with are patient credit balances and unidentified remittances. Although you may have an unusually large Lost and Found box, most of this tangible personal property is not reportable (see Chapter 7). While companies in the health care field are subject to the same unclaimed property laws as other industries, there are some special circumstances that may exclusively affect these types of businesses.

One trend in the health care industry that can cause a spike in reportable unclaimed property is the merger of smaller health care facilities and doctors' offices into larger hospital systems. This usually results in the centralization of accounting functions as well as the reissuance of account numbers that accompany most mergers. Patient and vendor account numbers can change and, in some cases, the data and relevant contact information can be lost in the shuffle. For example, patient credit balances transferred to a new account numbering system may not have the date that the credit was originally issued or correctly transferred. All of the credits may be mistakenly listed by the date that they were transferred to the new accounting system. If these data transfer mistakes are not caught and corrected before data from the old accounting or recordkeeping systems are destroyed, these credits may become unclaimed property without any way to perform due diligence or apply the credits to outstanding balances. As the credit balances have incorrect issuance dates listed, it can also create exposure for unclaimed property, as the holding periods will be incorrect and the new entity will probably not report the outstanding balances within the correct dormancy period. If an auditor sees that a company has merged, he or she will ask for the old records to check for just these types of discrepancies. The only way to detect these problems in advance is to perform extensive testing of the new accounting systems against the old systems, but in reality, there may not be enough personnel or time to complete all of the testing. Just be aware that these types of issues can result from big transfers of data to new systems and try to plan your unclaimed property internal reviews accordingly.

Even without a merger or consolidation, patient credit balances can be a nightmare for health facilities and their unclaimed property departments. Unlike most other businesses, in the health care industry, bills for one patient are often paid by multiple parties. Patients generally have at least one, if not two, insurance companies that make payments on patient accounts, and patients generally have to pay for at least some of their care themselves, through their contractually arranged co-payment plans. When someone overpays for patient care, there may be questions about who should actually receive the refund. It could be due to the patient who overpaid a bill while waiting to get notification of the amount that their insurance company would pay, or it could be due to the insurance company that overpaid for a service or paid for the same service twice because of overlapping invoices in their system. Maybe the patient was a self-pay customer, but later negotiated their rate for services down with the billing department after they had already paid a great deal of their bill. Whatever the cause, it is often not clear which party should be reimbursed when patient accounts have a credit balance.

It is often necessary to consult the payment contracts that the hospitals have with insurance companies to see if they have agreed to reimburse overpayments. If the issue cannot be resolved, the refund will probably go to the patient whose name is on the account. When you are looking at the issue from an unclaimed property point of view, the date that the credit was issued is important for tracking dormancy. You should have a protocol in your policy and procedure manual for researching patient credits to determine which party on the account should receive the refund. If the matter cannot be resolved, the most conservative approach would be to report the credit in the name of the patient, but you should definitely discuss the matter with your legal counsel to determine the approach that is best for your facility. Do not forget that B2B exemptions may apply if the credits are due to the insurance company, rather than to the patient!

Everyone who has visited a doctor or hospital lately has certainly been asked to read and sign some type of privacy notice and release of records permission for their health care provider. Even if we do not know what HIPAA means (Health Insurance Portability and Accountability Act), we have all been inundated with the acronym during the past decade. With the onset of HIPAA[7] regulations, the health care industry has faced increasing problems both with keeping confidential patient data secure when performing due diligence as required under the federal regulations and transmitting the data to the states in a secure manner to ensure the same level of patient privacy. The purpose of HIPAA was to improve the efficiency and effectiveness of the health care system by encouraging the development of a secure health information system that would simplify electronic transmission of certain health-related patient data. The Department of Health and Human Services added privacy and security requirements to HIPAA after the Act was made law. The privacy and security safeguards include Transaction and Code Set Standards, Privacy Standards, Security Standards, and Identifier Standards. HIPAA rules and regulations apply to every health plan, health care clearinghouse, or health care provider that conducts certain health care transactions electronically. HIPAA can also bind any third-party business associate of one of these covered entities that might performs service for them.

To be a business associate for purposes of HIPAA, a third party can be any nongovernmental person or company with which the covered entity shares covered information (including patient information) which is not a member of the covered entity's workforce. This can include another person or company that deals with payments or health care operations, or someone providing legal, actuarial, accounting, consulting, financial, administrative, or management services for a HIPAA-covered entity. This means that if your company does business with a HIPAA-covered entity, you may be subject to the same limitations with certain sensitive information that they are.

Without going into an exhaustive discussion of the impact that meeting these HIPAA requirements can have on your business, let us just talk about how your unclaimed property program might be influenced. You may run into HIPAA concerns when you are performing due diligence. Your letter, although probably not transmitted electronically, may contain confidential medical information that violates your HIPAA requirements if you do not word it correctly. For example, say that you are a psychiatric hospital. If you have received an overpayment from a patient for medical services rendered, you will probably issue them a credit. If they do not receive further medical treatment from your facility and do not request reimbursement, your facility will be holding reportable unclaimed property for this former patient. When the time comes to write the due diligence letter, you will have to keep all of the HIPAA privacy requirements in mind. If you out-source your due-diligence efforts, your outsource provider may fall under HIPAA's definition of business associate and will have to be expressly educated on how to prevent exposure.

If your due diligence efforts go unanswered and you have to report HIPAA-related transactions as unclaimed property, you will be exposing your company to another potential violation if you are not careful. As some states require holders to file their reports electronically, your filings will have to meet HIPAA standards for the electronic transmission of medical information. The information that state unclaimed property administrators want you to include in your unclaimed property report may be just the type of information that HIPAA does not want you to publish outside of the HIPAA-regulated group. You should speak to the state unclaimed property offices where you file to discuss the confidenti-ality of the patient information that you are responsible for safeguarding. You may have to consider removing or masking patient names before providing unclaimed property data if the state databases are not properly secured.

Under HIPAA, the reports that you send electronically will also have to be properly encrypted. If you outsource your compliance, your unclaimed property compliance provider will also have to meet HIPAA's encryption requirements to prevent you from having exposure. You may also have to get your unclaimed property compliance provider to sign the HIPAA business associates contract to ensure that they are aware of the obligations that go along with handling sensitive information and to obligate them to provide the correct safeguards. HIPAA's reach can be very broad, and your institution may bear the brunt of the repercussions if you and your business associates cannot properly secure private patient data while performing your unclaimed property obligations.

Not-for-Profit Medical Service Providers

With a few notable exceptions, charitable organizations, even hospitals, are subject to the same unclaimed property reporting requirements as other entities. One of these rare exemptions exists for Internal Revenue Code §501(c)(3) hospitals, or hospitals run by a county or municipal government in the state of Ohio.[8] Even this exemption, in its very exemption language, requires that the potentially exempt entity make a good-faith effort to perform due diligence or it will not be exempt from the rest of the unclaimed property compliance requirements. Not much of an exemption, is it? For the most part, charitable medical service providers will have to perform the same type of unclaimed property efforts as the rest of us.

OIL, GAS, UTILITIES, AND ENERGY

The oil and gas industries, the coal mining industry, the energy industry, and utilities are some of the most heavily regulated industries in the United States. They are taxed heavily and are plagued by customers who are constantly moving and changing. These unique industries also have some unique unclaimed property problems.

Oil, Gas, Coal Mining, and Other Mineral Mining Industries

Oil and gas companies and coal and mineral mining are often plagued by various sorts of unclaimed payments that they must track for unclaimed property purposes. For ease of discussion, I am going to refer to all of these types of industries as "oil and gas." These companies make a lot of payments arising from contractual obligations related to mineral property use and the lease and purchase of mineral rights. A mineral interest is, essentially, ownership of real property. As such, state unclaimed property laws generally do not attempt to regulate or claim underlying mineral interests, even if they are abandoned under the law. States *do,* however, become interested once ongoing or periodic payments arising from the sale of minerals or the development of mineral properties become abandoned. Mineral proceeds are broadly defined in most states' laws to include any payments generated from the production and sale of minerals, payments to nonoperators of mineral producing property under a joint operating agreement, or payments associated with the acquisition and retention of mineral leases. Some specific examples of mineral proceeds are royalties, ORRI (overriding royalties interest), shut-in royalties, production payments, lease bonuses, minimum royalties, and delay rentals. These payments are all potential unclaimed property for oil and gas companies. Some other areas of unclaimed property for the oil and gas industry are more typical, like payroll, accounts payable, accounts receivable, equity (including stocks, dividends, and debentures) and downstream operations payments associated with processing and refining.

The frequency of well and lease trading, as well as the proliferation of mergers and acquisitions, in the oil and gas industry leads to a lot of lost and abandoned well interests. Owner information is often lost in the shuffle of these sales, especially if the well or lease at issue has been closed for some time. Royalty checks and other payments are also often held for long periods of time for legitimate reasons, such as title disputes or unpaid amounts due from royalty owners on other properties.

Some states, like Texas and Oklahoma, have very specific unclaimed property laws related to the oil and gas industry. Oklahoma, for example, has laws that require forced pooling of mineral interests. This law was developed to ensure that oil production takes place at a rate that will recover the most oil, instead of haphazardly, as in the old days of big gushing wells. If you have been force-pooled in a state like Colorado or Oklahoma, and you are doing the drilling, you will probably have a load of royalty checks to pay to the other members of your pool. The unclaimed property administrator will be looking for you to report the unclaimed royalty checks, as well as any bonus payments or other payments relating to pooled shares. You may also come up against reporting problems when ownership interests in your pool have been abandoned and sold, per the law. You would generally receive ownership information from the state government for members of your pool at the time it was created. These lists may become unreliable over time as these owners disappear or die, especially if you have capped a well and not issued checks for a period of time, but then reopen the well and restart operations.

The good news is that, in states where the oil and gas industry is large, the instructions for filling out unclaimed property reports will often include specific instructions for this industry. The bad news is that the unclaimed property due for mineral interests will be treated differently than the other types of unclaimed property that you are tracking. These amounts due are generally handled under the *current pay* or *current balance* theory, meaning that once the first outstanding payment due to an owner reaches the state's minimum dormancy period and becomes reportable, you should report *all* of the funds due to that lost owner at one time, even current balances that are not yet considered unclaimed under the state's unclaimed property laws. It does not matter whether there are one or one hundred abandoned checks sitting on your books; you are to report all of the funds as one lump sum and then send all payments each year thereafter that the owner continues to be lost or unreachable. There are 23 current pay states,[9] and it would behoove you to review them each separately, as their holding periods for the first transaction to become dormant vary.

Even if you do not have current ownership information, old funds due and owing to the owners of the abandoned interest will have to be reported to the unclaimed property department. When the interest is sold, the new owner is probably only entitled to the funds that became due and owing after the date of their purchase. Under the unclaimed property laws, any old royalties, bonus payments, or other payments would still be the property of the previous owner and would be held for them until they were claimed by them, their heirs, or assigns from the unclaimed property administration.

Utilities

The utility industry has many of the same unclaimed property issues as the rest of the business world, with the exception of dealing routinely with unclaimed customer deposits and credits. Utility companies, as a practice, require deposits from customers before they will begin servicing new accounts. While the purpose of these deposits is to cover costs for account holders who damage utility property or do not pay their bills, these funds are often forgotten about by customers who could have them returned when they cancel their service with the utility company. Some people move without providing a forwarding address or close accounts where direct deposits could be made. Many customers *do* provide a forwarding address for their final bill, but do not contact the utility when their final statement shows a credit due to them. Many utility companies do not, as a rule, automatically issue refund checks for customers unless they are contacted and asked to do so. If these former customers do not contact the utility, the utility company is forced, under the unclaimed property laws, to report that unclaimed credit or uncashed deposit refund check to the appropriate unclaimed property office. Since we are such a mobile society, a local utility might have property due to 20 or more states, according to the last known addresses that they have on their books for former customers. Even the smallest utility company can have a huge unclaimed property compliance problem. Do not ignore the problem, because more and more states are putting utility companies on their audit short lists.

Utility Co-ops

While utilities generally have to file the same unclaimed property reports as other businesses, some states have exempted utility co-ops from having to report unclaimed property as long as they use the abandoned funds for some purpose that supports the common interests of the utility cooperative's local community. These exemptions still require the co-ops to attempt to do due diligence and find the owners, but if this fails, the co-op can use the money for the benefit of the cooperative members instead of turning the funds over to the state at-large. In Wisconsin, for example, unclaimed patronage refunds from the 66 Wisconsin Electric co-ops go to fund a charity for local youth. Since co-ops exist only to keep energy costs down for a specific group of people, and they are owned by these members, it only seems fair that unclaimed funds go back into the group of owners. Did I mention that some part of the unclaimed property law was actually fair to businesses? How unusual!

Retail

The retail industry is one of the most competitive lines of business. Besides sales and competitive pricing, retailers are always on the lookout for the hook that will keep customers coming through their doors. Many of these programs can cause unclaimed property problems. Rebates have long been a source of unclaimed property problems, and now *received not invoiced* property is becoming the focus of many auditors' efforts. We will discuss a few areas that are frequently the focus of auditors.

Customer Loyalty/Incentive Programs

Older programs like layaways and rebate checks are being replaced by customer loyalty programs that enable customers to accumulate reward points to be redeemed for merchandise certificates. There is still some question surrounding whether or not these unused incentive program points or the unredeemed gift certificates issued as prizes are escheatable. The laws in most states are only concerned with collecting unclaimed property that is based on an underlying debt. As most incentive programs are based on earning rewards or gifts, and no service is performed or money exchanged, these items are seen as charitable in nature and it could be logically argued that they are *not subject to escheat.* The way that your loyalty program is structured may alter this assumption, however. It would be a good idea to have your legal counsel review the terms of your program to ensure that you are not crossing the line into the world of escheatable property.

Gift Certificates/Gift Cards

The most obvious unclaimed property issue for retailers right now is the treatment of gift certificates and gift cards. I do not think that I know of a single retail establishment that does not offer some sort of gift certificate, gift card, electronic gift certificate, or all of the above. While layaways used to create unclaimed property headaches if the payments were not completed and the merchandise was never picked up by the customer, so unredeemed gift cards, with their 10% breakage or rate of nonredemption, plague retailers today. Since we have already discussed gift cards at length in Chapter 7, I will not go over everything again here, but it is important to note that you can make a real impact on changing state laws to have gift certificates exempted from unclaimed property collection by contacting lawmakers and lobbying to have gift cards exempted from unclaimed property reporting. It seems to be a trend to exempt gift cards and gift certificates from the unclaimed property laws, but be cautioned that consumer protection groups are also working hard to protect the rights of consumers to use these gifts in their own time. A lot of retailers have stopped waiting for the lawmakers to take a stand and have begun issuing gift cards that never expire, never impose a service charge, and never have any administrative fees. This certainly solves at least one of their unclaimed property problems.

NOTES

1. See, for example, *Aetna Cas. & Sur. Ins. Co. v. State,* 414 So. 2d 455 (Ala. 1982); *Allstate Ins. Co. v. Eagerton,* 403 So. 2d 172 (Ala. 1981); *Kane v. Insurance Company of North America,* 392 A.2d 325.
2. See, for example, *Blue Cross of N. Cal. v. Cory,* 120 Cal. App. 3d 723 (Cal. Ct. App. 1981); *Revenue Cabinet v. Blue Cross & Blue Shield of Ky., Inc.,* 702 S.W.2d 433 (Ky. 1986).
3. *N. Carolina State Treasurer v. City of Asheville,* 300 S.E.2d 283 (N.C. App. 1983) (state unable to prove that unpresented Elvis tickets were truly unclaimed); *Broussard v. Louisiana Public Service Commission,* No. 89-CA-0964 (La. 1989) (state unable to prove that the remainder of the refund reserve was payable); *Mason Dixon Lines v. Eagerton,* 555 F. Supp. 434 (M.D. Ala. 1982) (state unable to prove that customer and interline credits were "unqualifiedly due" anyone); and *Kane v. Insurance Company of North America,* 394 A.2d 325 (Pa. Common. Ct. 1978) (state failed to prove that claimants were "unqualifiedly entitled" to insurance proceeds).
4. *Insurance Co. of North America v. Knight,* 8 Ill. App. 3d 871, 291 N.E.2d 40 (4th Dist. 1972). The ruling in the *Knight* case was also specifically written into the Uniform Unclaimed Property Act of 1995 §6.
5. In 1999, several senior executives, along with Banker's Trust itself, were prosecuted when state auditors found flagrant and widespread abuse of unclaimed property by the bank. Banker's Trust falsified documents and lied about the unclaimed property it had in its possession. With the full knowledge of some of its executives, the bank falsified accounting records and took unclaimed property into miscellaneous income to make it appear as if the escheatable funds were profits instead of liabilities, which is a violation of general state unclaimed property laws. The fine paid by Banker's Trust was more than $50 million and a restatement of their financial statements. Sarbanes-Oxley problems? You bet!
6. 12 U.S.C. §§2501-2503 (1976).

7. HIPAA refers to the Administrative Simplification provisions of the Health Insurance Portability and Accountability Act of 1996 (HIPAA, Title II), which required the Department of Health and Human Services (HHS) to establish national standards for electronic health care transactions and national identifiers for providers, health plans, and employers. It also addressed the security and privacy of health data. (From www.hipaa.org, a Web site administered by the U.S. Government Department of Health and Human Services).

8. Oh Rev. Code §169.01(d)(2); *holder* does not mean any hospital granted tax-exempt status under section 501(c)(3) of the Internal Revenue Code or any hospital owned or operated by the state or by any political subdivision. Any entity, to be exempt from the definition of *holder* pursuant to this division, shall make a reasonable, good-faith effort to contact the owner of the unclaimed funds.

9. The oil and gas current pay states include: Alabama, Alaska, Arizona, Arkansas, Connecticut, Indiana, Kansas, Louisiana, Maine, Massachusetts, Montana, Nebraska, New Jersey, New Mexico, North Carolina, North Dakota, Ohio, Oklahoma, Texas, Utah, Vermont, West Virginia, and Wyoming.

CHAPTER 9

Foreign Unclaimed Property Laws

Just when you think that you have all of your transactions properly separated into the correct reporting states, you run into some foreign transactions. You have some outstanding unclaimed checks or credits, and the last known address in your records is in a country other than the United States or its territories. Where do you escheat the funds? Do you have to perform due diligence? The answer is . . . it depends. Since the priority rules of *Texas v. New Jersey* do not discuss unclaimed funds with last known addresses outside of the United States and its territories, you should refer to the unclaimed property laws in your state of incorporation for guidance. Any foreign address transactions will be subject to escheat (or not) depending on the law of your domicile state. The states are not consistent in their treatment of this situation, and there is no overriding federal legislation or case law to provide guidance.

The 1954 and 1966 Uniform Unclaimed Property Acts did not directly mention unclaimed foreign address property. The 1981 and 1995 Acts said that the Act "does not apply to any property held, due and owing in a foreign country and arising out of a foreign transaction."[1] The language in the Uniform Acts seems to deal only with entirely foreign transactions. Section 3(5) of the 1981 Act and Section 4(5) of the Uniform Act seem to address transactions where the holder is a U.S. company, but the owner is located in a foreign country. These sections say that the state of the holder's incorporation should take custody of property where the address of the true owner is in a foreign nation. The Supreme Court and Congress have not dealt with the issue of foreign-address unclaimed property. We are left with the laws of the states where our companies are incorporated for the little bit of guidance that they provide.

There are basically three camps when it comes to escheating foreign unclaimed funds. The first camp follows the directives of the 1981 and 1995 Uniform Unclaimed Property Acts and takes the position that property with an address outside of the United States and its territories should, by default, be reported to the state of the holder's corporate domicile.[2] The second camp completely excludes foreign address property from unclaimed property reporting or collection.

The third camp contains the few states that have not addressed foreign transactions at all in any form of legislation or administrative guidance. Delaware, for example, did not adopt any of the model legislation or even specifically address foreign transactions in its statutes. They do, however, define a holder as "any person having possession, custody or control of the property of another person and includes every (other) legal entity incorporated or created under the laws of this state or doing business in this state."[3] Even though they do not specifically address foreign transactions, the all-encompassing definitions seem to include all unclaimed property, no matter where the last known address of the apparent owner is located. The state of Delaware will audit for an attempt to collect foreign address unclaimed property, whether their laws make it clear that they can or not. Unless the state where you are incorporated specifically exempts foreign address property, just assume that you will have to report it to them. If you are not sure, you will need to carefully read the filing instructions for the unclaimed property report in your state of incorporation. If you are still not clear, call the unclaimed property office in your state and ask for guidance. Do not be surprised if they tell you that they want the foreign address property.

U.S. Laws on Foreign Escheat

Indian Reservations

While they are technically located on U.S. soil and within the boundaries of several states, Indian reservations are subject to tribal ordinances rather than state laws. An Indian tribal reservation is considered a sovereign entity, separate and apart from the laws of the state or territory where it is geographically located. The 50 states have no jurisdiction over these reservations, but the tribes are subject to federal jurisdiction. As most of the body of unclaimed property is state law, the unclaimed property laws generally do not apply to Indian reservations. As such, states have not tried to escheat from any of the Indian tribes, although they may be holding property for them. As a practical matter, I would suggest that you send any property belonging to members of an Indian tribe to the state unclaimed property office where the reservation is located, out of courtesy. If you would prefer, however, there is really nothing stopping you from following the instructions of your state of incorporation for the treatment of foreign transactions when dealing with property belonging to an apparent true owner who is located on an Indian reservation.

U.S. Territories

While the three U.S. territories do not have all of the rights apparent to the states, they do have unclaimed property laws. Guam, Puerto Rico, and the U.S. Virgin Islands all have reports and collect unclaimed property, but certainly not to the extent that the 50 states and the District of Columbia audit and collect unclaimed funds.

Guam   The unclaimed property statues in Guam deal only with dormant bank accounts. Savings accounts have a dormancy period of ten years, checking accounts have a dormancy period of two years (during which there is no interest accrual) and other unidentified deposits and loan payments have a dormancy period of three years. Guam provides for true escheat under their laws. Banks must attempt to perform due diligence. Any unclaimed funds are turned over to the Treasurer of Guam, who holds the property in trust for true owners to recover for five years; no interest accrues on the property. The funds become the property of the territorial government if they are not claimed within five years from the date that they are turned over. It is interesting to note that Guam is a bifurcated report and remit government, with reports due on October 1 of one year and the dormant moneys paid during the month of January of the following year.[4]

Puerto Rico   Puerto Rico has an extensive body of unclaimed property law contained in its Abandoned or Unclaimed Money and Other Liquid Assets Act.[5] The unclaimed property laws of Puerto Rico deal with financial institutions and other holders, which are defined to mean "any person that in the course of his business has in his custody money or other liquid assets belonging to another person, with the obligation of returning or paying them to said other person, his beneficiaries, heirs, or successors in law, on a specific date or one to be determined, or when a certain or contingent event occurs, whether foreseeable or not."[6] In general, all unclaimed funds have a five-year dormancy period, and there is no anti-limitations provision, which means that, despite the expiration of a statute of limitations to sue for payment of certain items such as checks, this does not affect the running of the dormancy period. This means that even though someone cannot sue to have a check returned to them after three years, the holder may still be bound to report the property after five years have passed.

Puerto Rican law also requires holders to publish notification of abandoned property worth more than $100 in their local newspaper of general circulation, but it does not require that they publish this notice in the apparent true owner's local newspaper. If the holder is in Washington, D.C., he or she only has to publish notification of property belonging to individuals in Puerto Rico in their local D.C. newspaper. This would seem to defeat the purpose of advertising! Unclaimed property reports are due on August 10 for all property deemed dormant as of the previous June 30. Holders have to report all property in Puerto Rico worth more than $1, and there is no policy for aggregation. The government of Puerto Rico holds unclaimed funds for apparent owners for an unlimited amount of time, and they even pay interest at the rate of 4% per year when owners claim their property. It is also interesting to note that Puerto Rican law allows the government to hire third-party contractors to recover unclaimed funds when deemed necessary. As all of the laws and forms in Puerto Rico are published in Spanish, its official government language, you may have to request an English translation of the forms and instructions that you need from the government unclaimed property office to properly defend your audit. You may also need a translator to write your due diligence letters in Spanish and then translate any responses you receive.

U.S. Virgin Islands   The U.S. Virgin Islands have adopted the Uniform Unclaimed Property Act of 1981. They generally have a five-year dormancy period for almost all types of property. Their unclaimed property report is due on November 1 of each year for property that became due and owing during the period of July 31 of the previous year to June 30 of the current year. They allow holders to aggregate property worth less than $25, but they only require holders to perform due diligence and send letters to the last known address of owners with property worth more than $50.

If you have an unclaimed property software package, you will assuredly have the necessary unclaimed property reports for these U.S. territories, but reports are not yet available on their state Web sites. All forms for Puerto Rico are published in Spanish, and you have to contact the government offices to get copies of forms and laws translated into English. You can find the contact information for these offices at www.naupa.org under the *resources: links* section.

OTHER NATIONS' LAWS

As discussed earlier in this chapter, the unclaimed property laws of the various states dictate how we treat unclaimed funds where the address of the apparent true owner is outside of the United States. We only have to follow these directions, however, if the funds are truly abandoned and we have not either returned the funds to the true owner or reported them to some other custodial government. Like the United States, the only foreign nations that seem to address the issue of unclaimed funds are the United Kingdom or nations that were formerly governed by the United Kingdom. Here is a brief overview of the unclaimed property laws of other countries. If you have occasion to do business with citizens or businesses in these other countries, it may be a good business practice to attempt to follow their unclaimed property rules for any outstanding transactions you may have with their citizens.

Canada

Canada has been developing both national and regional unclaimed property regulations in the recent past. Bank accounts have been specifically addressed in its national law, and the provinces have either established unclaimed property laws, in the case of British Columbia and Quebec, or are in the development stages, as with Alberta. While none of the provinces in Canada are auditing for unclaimed property, they do appreciate voluntary compliance with their laws.

British Columbia As of April 1, 2000, the former escheat law, the Unclaimed Money Act, was repealed and replaced by the Unclaimed Property Act. The unclaimed property of British Columbians is administered by the British Columbia Unclaimed Property Society. Both the British

Columbia Unclaimed Property Society and nongovernment organizations are required to make reasonable efforts to reunite owners with their unclaimed property. The major difference between these laws and the average U.S. state law is that the holder is generally responsible for keeping track of unclaimed property in British Columbia, rather than the government. As of July 1, 2000, if property becomes unclaimed under the law, a holder is required to make reasonable efforts to locate the owner of the property. If unsuccessful within six months of making reasonable efforts, the holder must post the name of the owner on a public database. This legislation is not retroactive and applies only to transactions occurring after July 1, 2000.

Under the British Columbia Unclaimed Property Act, property becomes unclaimed when an owner leaves property (such as financial assets) with no instruction, no claim, and no transaction for certain periods of time. The British Columbia Unclaimed Property Act applies if the last known address of the apparent true owner was in British Columbia and if the transaction that gave rise to the property was entered into after July 1, 2000. The legislation also applies if the owner's address is unknown and the transaction from which the property arose was entered into or arranged in British Columbia after July 1, 2000. Generally, the legislation requires property to be classified as unclaimed after three years of inactivity, with some exceptions. One notable exception occurs when a letter or check is sent to the owner and returned undeliverable to the holder. As soon as the holder receives the returned check, the property becomes unclaimed.

Holders in British Columbia are permitted to charge service fees for administering unclaimed property, provided that they have these fees written into their contracts with owners. Holders may not charge an owner for the cost of making reasonable efforts to locate them and notify them of their property. However, holders may already have service contracts related to the property, and the law does not interfere with those contractual relationships. In addition, the law does not prohibit a holder from establishing reasonable fees for processing a claim. The fee should be set in relation to the cost of processing a claim. Under certain circumstances, holders can petition the government of British Columbia to take custody of unclaimed funds if they have already taken all of the required due diligence steps and the funds are still unclaimed by the true owner.

Québec   The law regarding when property becomes unclaimed in Québec is similar to unclaimed property laws in the United States. Unclaimed property is generally limited to financial assets; the law does not seem to address abandoned tangible personal property, such as items that are not financial documents that might be abandoned in a safe-deposit box. Property covered by the unclaimed property law is considered to be unclaimed when the owner has not made a claim, performed a transaction, or provided instructions with respect to the asset for a period of three years after it becomes cashable or payable. To be covered by the unclaimed property law, the asset must belong to an untraceable owner whose last known address was in Québec. The law also covers assets that were acquired in Québec by a person for whom there is no known address, or that may belong to a person resident in a jurisdiction where there are no unclaimed property laws.

Businesses in Québec holding unclaimed financial assets are required to send a notice to the owners after three years of inactivity. If the owners do not respond, or if the institutions holding the assets are unable to contact the owners, the institutions are required to remit such assets to Revenu Québec once a year. These businesses are also required to maintain records at their offices of all of the assets remitted to Revenu Québec. These assets must remain on the list for ten years, in case a true owner or their assign makes a claim on the property. There is *no* time limit for owners or assigns to claim and recover financial assets remitted to Revenu Québec, except for amounts worth less than $500 and amounts that were remitted to the Minister of Finance before July 1, 1999. In the latter case, the time limit is ten years.

Alberta   In early 2007, the Alberta Legislature introduced Bill 41, entitled the Unclaimed Personal Property and Vested Property Act. The types of potentially unclaimed property covered by Bill 41 include: dividend and interest payments; funds from redemptions and other forms of distribution; security certificates and other evidences of ownership; and bonds, debentures, and other evidences of indebtedness. While the legislature has ended the period where it solicited comments on the bill from the public, it has not yet been enacted into law, although lawmakers are hopeful that it will be enacted in 2008.[7]

United Kingdom

The original source of our unclaimed property laws operates a very limited escheat program today. It is surprising, really; the *Financial Times,* a respected London newspaper, reported that the entire amount of unclaimed property in Great Britain, Scotland, and Wales is estimated to be worth £77 billion, but most of that is still in the hands of the banks and insurance companies to be claimed by British citizens, rather than being used by the government, as in the United States. These numbers are just estimates, however, since banks and other institutions holding unclaimed funds in the United Kingdom are not required to report the amounts they are holding or to turn the abandoned funds over to the British government. The United States is much more aggressive in its unclaimed property collections. The National Association of Unclaimed Property Administrators estimated that the states, in total, are holding over $10 billion in unclaimed funds.

At the national level, the Commission on Unclaimed Assets administers only a few property types for British citizens. The laws deal mostly with dormant bank or building society accounts and insurance policies. Both property types have long dormancy periods compared to those in the United States. A dormant bank account is transferred to a reserve account where it earns no interest after one to three years, but the banks and building societies have to hold the property without using it for their own benefit for a total of 15 years. Insurance policies have a 15-year dormancy period and are listed in an Insured Pensions registry.

The majority of the lost money in the United Kingdom comes from dormant bank accounts, but the unclaimed funds are also made up of orphan pensions; missing shares and abandoned dividends; forgotten life insurance policies; National Savings Certificates; and Premium Bonds that have not been redeemed. Also included is £300 million in unclaimed National Lottery winnings. Once property reaches its full dormancy, it can be used again by the bank. There is no government reporting requirement, and the banks do not have to disclose the amount of money that they are holding. Banks are supposed to write to their lost investors at least once a year, according to the British Banking Code, but if the mail is returned, most banks stop writing. If a person shows up to reclaim lost funds, the banks have to return the money, plus reinstate the interest. Most claims can be made in perpetuity, but there are some exceptions. At the national level, there is legislation in place to deal with abandoned securities, which generally have a 12-year dormancy period before any action is taken by the company that issued the shares and gets to return them to its treasury once they are fully dormant.

In March 2007, the British government, with the support of the bank and building society sector, launched a study on the operation of a program aimed at reuniting unclaimed assets lying dormant in bank and building society accounts with their owners to reinvest into society those assets that remain unclaimed. The moneys would be transferred from the banks that are holding them to a centralized government agency that would distribute the money to different areas of the country to use for the benefit of various children's charities. The program would not be a true escheat, however, since the law will preserve a right for customers to reclaim their assets at any time, even after the law has been enacted. This new proposed scheme was published before the House of Lords in November 2007 with support from the government and is expected to go forward in the near future. In the meantime, though, it is business as usual.

Australia

Australia has one of the most extensive unclaimed property collection and administration regimes outside the United States. Unlike the United States, however, Australia has a combination of both national and local laws governing the administration of unclaimed property. *Unclaimed moneys* laws are not consistent or uniform across all jurisdictions, and the local state or territorial laws can be preempted by the passage of applicable national laws at any time.

Bank Accounts   There is a seven-year dormancy period for all unclaimed and abandoned accounts, pursuant to the Banking Act of 1954. Banks in Australia are required to report unclaimed property to the National Treasurer each year. The reports and the funds they cover are due to the Treasurer by March 31 each year, but they only have to report unclaimed accounts worth $500 or more. A list of the abandoned accounts is then published in the *Government Gazette*. Unlike in the United States, Australian owners must make claims to recover unclaimed property at the bank where the account was opened. The Treasury refunds the money to the bank, which passes it on to the claimant. The national government also maintains a searchable database on the Internet that can be found at: www.edge.asic. gov.au/unclaimed/simplequery.html.

Securities Under Commonwealth Corporations law, abandoned stock is reported to the Australian Securities Commission after a six-year dormancy period, while unclaimed dividends may be reported to individual Australian states. Companies are required to maintain a register available for public viewing, but the public has to pay a nominal fee to search the list. Australian corporations are required to enter the information for any shares that have reached the conclusion of their six-year dormancy period in the previous year by January 31 of each year. By March 31 each year, all of the information on accounts worth more than $10 is to be published in the Canberra Times and the Gazette. The unclaimed shares also have to be reported to the Registrar-General, but they are not turned over to the government quite yet. One year after publication, all unclaimed moneys are remitted to the Registrar-General.

If a public company has gone bankrupt or gone out of business, as of January 1, 1991, the law has set a six-month dormancy period. When this expires, all outstanding property vests in the Australian Securities Commission. Unclaimed moneys in the hand of liquidators for liquidations which took place before January 1, 1991 come under the jurisdiction of state or territorial authorities. The Australian government maintains a Web site, which can be accessed at www.asic.gov.au.

Pensions Unclaimed money held by retirement savings accounts providers are subject to the administration of the Registrar-General. As of June 30, 1997, trustees of pension accounts that are abandoned must submit reports twice a year, by October 31 and April 30 following each respective six-month period. The reports must include (1) name, gender, and date of birth of member/account holder; (2) last known address; (3) amount of money held; (4) name of last known employer; and (5) date of commencement of the policy/account. While this is a nationally administered program, there is a Registrar-General in each of the country's jurisdictions, with Web sites as follows:

- *Australian Capital Territories (ACT):* www.canberraconnect.act.gov.au
- *Queensland:* www.justice.qld.gov.au/births.htm
- *Tasmania:* www.justice.tas.gov.au/bdm/about_bdm.htm
- *Western Australia:* www.justice.wa.gov.au/birth/index.htm
- *Victoria:* www.justice.vic.gov.au
- *South Australia:* www.ocba.sa.gov.au/bdm/
- *New South Wales:* www.bdm.nsw.gov.au
- *Northern Territory:* www.ke.com.au/bdmaus/bdmnt/index.html

Salaries and Wages Unclaimed salaries and wages have a very short dormancy period in Australia. Employers are required to report unclaimed payroll in the relevant state or territory within 30 days after the termination of employment.

Legal Practitioners' Trust Accounts The Legal Practitioners Act of 1970 requires unclaimed moneys held in legal practitioners' trust accounts to be paid to the Registrar-General.

Real Estate Agents Trust Accounts The Agents Act of 1968 requires that unclaimed moneys held in agents' trust accounts be paid to the Registrar-General.

Other legislation dealing with abandoned funds varies by state/territory. While not legally bound to do so, the state or territory in which the company is incorporated generally holds unclaimed moneys.

Australian Capital Territory The unclaimed property laws specific to this area are very limited. The law states that the Public Trustee for the Australian Capital Territory (ACT) administers moneys in the ACT that have been declared unclaimed under the Unclaimed Moneys Act, the Legal Practitioners Act, and the Agents Act. Claim requirements differ under each of the three acts:

1. *Unclaimed Moneys Act.* Unclaimed moneys accounts include deposits, dividends, trust account funds, interest, refunds, overpayments, sale proceeds, bonds, superannuation benefits, and retirement savings

accounts that have been inactive for six years or more. Unclaimed money does not include bank, building society, and credit union accounts, which are payable to the Australian Securities and Investment Commission. Publication is required by the last day of March each year for all accounts worth $10 or more, both in a daily newspaper and in the *Government Gazette*. All funds that have not been paid within one year after publication are paid to the Public Trustee of Unclaimed Moneys within one month after the end of that year.

2. *Agents Act.* Unclaimed moneys under the Agents Act are trust moneys held by licensed agents for more than three years as declared unclaimed to the commissioner for fair trading.

3. *Legal Practitioners Act.* Unclaimed money under the Legal Practitioners Act consists of moneys held in trust accounts by solicitors for more than six years, where those entitled cannot be found or in cases where an individual has refused to accept the funds.

New South Wales   The local unclaimed property laws in New South Wales (NSW) seem only to deal with unclaimed estates of deceased persons. New South Wales passed the Unclaimed Money Act of 1995, whereby the Office of State Revenue, Unclaimed Moneys Unit is the contact for any of these types of issues. The NSW Public Trustee administers estates where next of kin and or beneficiaries cannot be located. Generally these proceeds are held for six years, and then paid to the NSW Treasury as unclaimed funds.[8] Any other unclaimed funds are still subject to Australian national laws, such as the ones for abandoned stock or wages.

Northern Territories   The Northern Territories have a few local unclaimed property laws. They enacted the Unclaimed Asset Moneys Act which requires that companies create an updated list of all of the unclaimed funds that they are holding and make that list available to the public for inspection by January 31 each year. Companies are also required to publish the list before the last day of February each year in the *Government Gazette*. All funds that have not been paid out within one year after publication in the *Gazette* must be paid to the treasurer with one month after the end of that year.

Queensland   Queensland also has its own local unclaimed funds law. The Public Trustee Act 1978–1981, Part VIII Unclaimed Property, sets a dormancy period of six years and seems, once again, to apply only to corporations. As a Valentine's Day gift, all corporations have to list all dormant account information on an Unclaimed Moneys Register by February 14 each year. Starting on February 15 and for a period of seven years thereafter, the register has to be open for public inspection at company headquarters for payment of $1. Names are advertised in the *Government Gazette* during month of February for all amounts over $50. All funds that have not been claimed within one year after publication are paid to the public trustee, but the company does get to recoup the cost of advertising in the *Government Gazette*. The state government promises that soon, a search feature will be available at the Public Trustee's unclaimed moneys Web site.

South Australia   South Australia has some of the oldest codified unclaimed laws in the world, outside of the Magna Carta in England. The Unclaimed Moneys Act of 1891 establishes a general dormancy period of six years. On January 1 of each year, companies are required to prepare a register including all unclaimed accounts worth more than $10. After January 8, the register is open for public inspection during business hours, for a payment not to exceed twenty cents. Companies also must publish account information in the South Australian *Government Gazette* annually during the month of January. All funds that have not been claimed within two years after the first publication of notice are paid to the Treasurer, minus costs of advertising.

Tasmania   Tasmania's law is also quite long standing. Pursuant to the Unclaimed Moneys Act of 1918, companies registered or doing business in Tasmania must make a register containing all unclaimed accounts available for publication on the last day of January each year. Publication is required in the *Government Gazette* by February 15. Funds remaining unclaimed 14 days prior to the expiration of a one-year period after publication are paid to the Treasurer, less advertising expenses.

Victoria   Victoria's law is meant to cover *all* unclaimed funds, no matter how small the amount. Under the Unclaimed Moneys Act of 1993, all sums of money whatsoever that have remain unpaid for at least 12 months are considered dormant. After March 8 of each year, information on all accounts must be made available to the public at company headquarters, without the company charging any sort of viewing fee like in the other states and territories. Advertisement in the *Government Gazette* during the month of March is required for accounts worth $10 or more. All funds that have not been claimed within 14 days of the one year anniversary of publication go to the Receiver of Revenue.

Western Australia   Bank accounts are given a longer dormancy period in Western Australia than in anywhere else in the world with unclaimed property laws. The Unclaimed Money Act of 1990 establishes a general dormancy period of six years for almost all property, except for interest bearing accounts, which are permitted 25 years of inactivity. When property reaches its full dormancy it is turned over the Consolidated Revenue Fund.

Companies in Western Australia also are required to report their unclaimed property. No later than January 31 of each year, companies must notify the Treasurer of dormant accounts and the owner information that they have on record, including the name, amount, and date of last activity. Not later than July 31, companies are required to notify the Treasurer of all accounts that have been claimed, after which advertisement must be made "as soon as practical" to ensure information is available to the public. This generally includes postings at government offices and police stations. Funds that remain unclaimed 14 days after advertisement must be paid to the Treasurer.

New Zealand

Unclaimed property law in New Zealand is published at a national level and is managed by the country's Inland Revenue Commission, which is the equivalent of the Internal Revenue Service in the United States. The laws are all centered on the Unclaimed Money Act 1971. The Act was put into law to ensure that people or organizations who hold funds on behalf of someone, either alive or deceased, take adequate steps to find the owners of unclaimed deposits and other amounts owing so that accounts can be cleared of unclaimed funds and, if the funds cannot be cleared, that the money is paid to the Crown (national government) to be used for the good of the community and/or returned to the true owner in the future. Once money has been paid into the Consolidated Account, true owners have to contact the Commissioner to reclaim any unclaimed funds being held on their behalf.

The Act is very thorough in its explanations of unclaimed property and how it is to be administered. It is almost as thorough as the Uniform Acts in the United States have been. The current unclaimed property law in New Zealand applies to transactions from June 1, 1971 forward and sets out the procedures to follow for holding, advertising, and reporting unclaimed money. It defines unclaimed money and holders of unclaimed money. Generally, money held in an account where there is no activity for six consecutive years (or 25 consecutive years, for some deposits) becomes unclaimed money. There are special provisions for amounts of $100 or less. Interestingly, there are three types of money that can never become unclaimed in New Zealand: (1) dividends (unless the company has been liquidated or the funds are dividends payable by mutual associations if the dividends are effectively interest on members, contributions, or deposits), (2) mutual association rebates, and (3) benefits payable from a pension or superannuation fund.

The Act applies to all companies, banks, building societies, insurance offices, moneylenders, auctioneers, real estate agents, accountants, sharebrokers, and motor vehicle dealers that hold defined classes of unclaimed money. There are special provisions where the holder has ceased to carry on business or has died. The Commissioner of Inland Revenue can also enter into special arrangements to exempt holders from some of the administrative requirements of the Act. The Act does not apply to certain types of unclaimed funds that are covered under other laws, like money held by attorneys in trust. Interestingly enough, the New Zealand law allows organizations or individuals who would not otherwise be subject to the laws to become holders voluntarily if they would like to get rid of the burden of administering unclaimed money.

In New Zealand, unclaimed money falls into three categories, each of which is administered differently: (1) deposits of money, (2) life insurance proceeds, and (3) certain types of trade debts. Money only becomes unclaimed money after it has been held for a certain length of time and it is situated in New Zealand. The Act declares that money unclaimed in another country is generally subject to that country's laws.

Holders of unclaimed money fall into one of three categories:

1. *General mandatory holders.* These are companies, banks, building societies, and insurance offices. General holders are liable to account for all classes of unclaimed money.

2. *Restricted mandatory holders.* There are certain holders (who are not companies) who are only obliged to account for particular kinds of unclaimed money. These holders, and the unclaimed money they must account for, are:
   - *Moneylenders.* Money they have borrowed in the course of the moneylending business
   - *Auctioneers.* The balance of any proceeds of goods sold at auction
   - *Real estate agents.* Money held in the real estate agent's trust account
   - *Sharebrokers.* Money held on behalf of clients
   - *Members of the New Zealand Society of Accountants.* Money held on behalf of clients
   - *Motor Vehicle Dealers.* Proceeds a dealer receives when acting as agent.

3. *Voluntary Holders.* Any person, firm, body, or institution not included in one of the previous definitions can elect to be a holder and comply with the provisions of the Act. For example, any person (or personal representative) may elect to be a holder when the business has ceased or death has occurred.

On June 1 of each year, holders must turn in a report, in alphabetical order, of all of the unclaimed money that reached its full dormancy in the preceding year. The holders have to make the register available for inspection by the public. By June 30 of each year, the holder must send a letter to each owner (at the last known address), providing details of the unclaimed money. By September 30 of each year, the holder has to report to the Commissioner of Internal Revenue all of the entries made in the register. If the money is not claimed by the owner, the holder must pay it to the Commissioner, as long as the funds are worth more than $100 for any one owner. If the amount of money due to one owner is worth less than $100, then the holder can decide whether or not it wants to report those funds.

Once properties are deemed unclaimed and are turned over to the Inland Revenue, the funds are paid into the Consolidated Account. The Act requires that the information provided about the reported unclaimed funds be kept strictly confidential, except for the publication of names of owners and the amounts of money that are being held as unclaimed property on their behalf. The law also allows the Commissioner of Inland Revenue to examine, at any time, any register kept by a holder and any accounts of the holder that relate to unclaimed money (this means an audit!). The auditors can require the holders to make corrections to their registers of unclaimed property if all of the unclaimed funds they are holding are not properly listed. There are even criminal penalties and prosecution for failure to follow the unclaimed property laws. It is a criminal offense for a holder to willfully or negligently fail to comply with the Act. Where the holder is a company, both the company and the executive officer who authorized or permitted the failure are open to prosecution, and the courts can impose a fine of up to $500 upon conviction *for each offense.*

Hong Kong

The unclaimed property laws in this former British outpost are scarce. The only references found to any type of regulated property discussed dormant bank accounts and lottery winnings. Since there are no specific disclosure or reporting rules regarding dormant bank accounts, the exact amount of unclaimed funds held by Hong Kong financial institutions is impossible to determine. Because most banks impose service fees after six months of inactivity and/or when the balance drops below $500, abandoned accounts are eventually depleted. Any remaining funds are generally forfeited, accounted for as miscellaneous income.

Hong Kong does make some attempt to regulate and collect unclaimed lottery winnings. The Hong Kong Jockey Club, which runs Mark Six lotteries, reported that unclaimed winning tickets total about $2.2 million per week, which is $115 million in an average year. The Hong Kong Lotteries Board recently decreased the forfeiture period for claiming lottery winnings from six months to sixty days. Unclaimed amounts go to the Social Welfare Department's Lottery Fund, which is used to support various charities including projects for the elderly and impoverished.

Hong Kong's government has an interesting practice for unclaimed over-payments of tax. In an average year, the Inland Revenue Commission turns over $12 million in excess taxes paid by residents and expatriates to the Treasury, where it is treated as general revenue. The Commission has a policy that it will refund overpayments if the true owner provides documentary proof, and it claims that the process is simple and uncomplicated, but is *anything* related to the government ever really simple or uncomplicated?

NOTES

1. UUPA of 1981, §36 and UUPA of 1995, §26. *Note:* The Commission that drafted the 1995 UUPA left the language of the 1981 UUPA section 36 the same, but renumbered the section as Section 26.
2. The following states have enacted the Uniform Unclaimed Property Act of 1981: Alaska, Colorado, District of Columbia, Florida, Georgia, Idaho, Iowa, Maryland, Michigan, Minnesota, Nevada, New Hampshire, New Jersey, North Dakota, Oklahoma, Oregon, Rhode Island, South Carolina, South Dakota, Tennessee, Utah, Vermont, Virginia, Washington, Wisconsin, and Wyoming. The following states have enacted the Uniform Unclaimed Property Act of 1995: Alabama, Arizona, Arkansas, Indiana, Kansas, Louisiana, Maine, Montana, New Mexico, North Carolina, and West Virginia.
3. Del. Code, Title 12, §1198(6).
4. 11 GCA §§ 106119, et al.
5. Rev. Juridica U.P.R. §§2101-2106.
6. Rev. Juridica U.P.R. §2101(f).
7. http://www.cibcmellon.com/Contents/en_CA/English/NewsRoom/Publications/Inform/2006/IN200611_02.html.
8. Ibid.

CHAPTER 10

Selected Legal Issues in Unclaimed Property Audits

One of the biggest problems that holders have with the current status of escheat law is that there is no single body of unclaimed property law applicable to all states. The so-called Uniform Acts have not been uniformly adopted, and each state and territory has its own quirks and special measures. As the number of multistate third-party auditors continues to grow, companies will be more and more likely to be the target of a multistate unclaimed property audit. Even though the laws of each of the states at issue may differ, these multistate audits are generally conducted as though either the 1981 or the 1995 Uniform Acts control all of the states. This can be costly for the holders being audited, especially if they are not familiar enough with the laws of each jurisdiction to realize that their assessments are not being calculated correctly. While it seems like an insurmountable goal to learn the laws of each of the jurisdictions, it is worthwhile to familiarize yourself with the general concepts that tend to be seen consistently through the body of escheat laws. We will discuss a few of the "universal" theories that may come up during an unclaimed property audit.

LACK OF NEXUS AS AN AUDIT DEFENSE

Even though we discussed the fact that unclaimed property laws are *not* taxes earlier in the book, it bears further discussion in this section. Many holders would like to be able to challenge a state's authority to conduct an unclaimed property audit on the basis that the company does not have *nexus,* or sufficient contacts with the state to allow that government to conduct such an intrusive audit. Unfortunately, the courts have continually denied relief to holders making this claim. Nexus is a tax concept that does not translate into the unclaimed property laws. The unclaimed property laws are based on the theory that the state has all of the rights and privileges of the true owner of unclaimed property. The courts in various cases have upheld the theory that states' claims are derived from the owners whose last known address was in their states, and the states can enforce these rights and recover property from holders under audit.[1] In legal circles, this is known as the *derivative rights doctrine*. The state, in claiming the right to demand custody of unclaimed or abandoned property, derives its rights from those of the missing owners of the property, as reflected on the books and records of holders. States cannot determine what property they should be protecting if they cannot examine the books and records of holders, and not all holders are going to voluntarily give that information to the various states, even though the law states that they should.

Courts have consistently held that states can audit for and recover unclaimed property from a holder even though the holder is not doing business in a state or otherwise subject to the state's jurisdiction. There are also reciprocal agreements among the states to collect and report property belonging to each other. What does all of this mean? Basically, it means that you are not going to be able to assert a lack of nexus on behalf of a state to keep them out of your books and records if they notify you that they are coming to conduct an unclaimed property audit.

DORMANCY FEES AND SERVICE CHARGES

While the derivative rights doctrine that we just discussed may hamper your right to prevent states from conducting an audit, it *can* help you to defend your own position on dormancy fees and service charges that you may impose to reduce the value of abandoned property.

Under the derivative rights doctrine, states claiming abandoned property only have rights and privileges to the extent that the true owner would have rights and privileges under the law. Unless they are specifically limited by statute, any defenses or set-offs that the holder would have against the true owner of the property can also be asserted against the states during an unclaimed property audit. The state laws generally recognize this in the statutory language of their catch-all provisions. The laws generally say something to the extent that the states can collect all intangible property, including any income or increment derived therefrom *less any lawful charges,* that is held, issued, or owing in the ordinary course of a holder's business and has remained unclaimed by the owner for more than a certain number of years after it became payable or distributable.

To assert this defense, however, the charges that you are imposing have to be lawful. The courts have held that lawful charges must generally meet two requirements: (1) the charge must be imposed pursuant to a valid and enforceable written agreement or other legal authority and (2) the charge must be enforced by the holder against all owners and not regularly waived or rescinded in practice. Some cases have refused to allow dormancy fees and service charges to offset otherwise reportable unclaimed property in cases where the true owner was not given sufficient explanation of the imposition of those fees or charges in advance. These decisions mean that printing a small brochure that is inconspicuously displayed and uses tiny print to explain potential service charges probably will be dismissed by an auditor as insufficient. Make sure that your legal department has thoroughly reviewed the unclaimed property laws and cases in this area so that they can help you construct your dormancy fee or service charge policy to be bulletproof under audit.

It is also important to note that consumer protection groups have been lobbying to have these sorts of charges prohibited on gift cards and the like in several states. Make sure that your account servicing fees or dormancy fees will not be struck down by some other aspect of the state law, even if they are not disallowed for purposes of unclaimed property administration.

EXPIRATION DATES AND OTHER CONTRACTUAL LIMITATION PERIODS

In general, the courts have continually held that parties to a contract may shorten the normal statute of limitations governing the enforcement of contracts if the periods of time that the parties agree on are reasonable. This general acceptance of contract limitations has been tempered by the caveat that the purpose of the provision cannot be solely for the purpose of avoiding unclaimed property laws. It is important to note that this type of provision has only been enforced against holders attempting to deny states from taking unclaimed property. There may still be a case for enforcing these types of contractual limitations against the true owners. Both the 1981 and the 1995 Uniform Acts removed contractual limitations as a defense to unclaimed property collection by stating that

> (t)he expiration, before or after the effective date of this [Act], of a period of limitation on the owner's right to receive or recover property, whether specified by contract, statute, or court order, does not preclude the property from being presumed abandoned or affect a duty to file a report or to pay or deliver or transfer property to the administrator as required by this [Act].[2]

This provision has also been widely affected by the states. What does this mean to you? If you have developed contractual language specifically to avoid escheating otherwise reportable property, you are probably not going to be able to defend that position under audit. If, however, you have contract terms that have legitimate business purposes and have the beneficial side effect of keeping property from becoming reportable, a court will probably uphold the language. The burden of proof will be on you, however, to prove that you did not institute expiration dates or contractual limitations just to avoid unclaimed property reporting. It is also important to note that your contract terms may be limited by statutes that have been enacted in some states to protect the public. Make sure that your language is up to date with any law changes that might have been made.

Unclaimed Employee Benefits

Here is an area where there is still a lot of controversy. The Department of Labor, which regulates federal pension plans, has consistently taken the position that the Employee Retirement Income Security Act of 1974 (also known as ERISA) preempts state abandoned property laws. States are still trying to collect abandoned employee benefits during unclaimed property audits. The U.S. Supreme Court has not yet heard or decided the issue, and the lower federal courts have reached conflicting decisions in different jurisdictions. How can you handle unclaimed employee benefits without bringing the wrath of either the federal or state governments down on your company? Good question! Just assume that federal laws trump state laws, including unclaimed property laws. If employee benefits are unclaimed, but are also subject to an ERISA plan, it would be safe to take the position that the federal law should be considered the correct law to follow. It is vital to look at the language of your particular employee benefits plan. If turning unclaimed funds in your employee benefit accounts over to any state government conflicts with the terms of the plan, I would not remit the money to any state unclaimed property office without a court order stating that I was to do so. Let us also hope that either the U.S. Supreme Court or the Congress decides this controversy for us in the near future.

UNCLAIMED PROPERTY OF BANKRUPT HOLDERS

Here is another area where federal law would seem to preempt state unclaimed property laws. According to the legal information Web site www.nolo.com, bankruptcy is described as *a federal court* process designed to help individuals and businesses eliminate their debts or repay them under the protection of the bankruptcy court. Bankruptcies can generally be described as liquidations or reorganizations. Chapter 7 bankruptcy is the liquidation variety—property is sold (liquidated) to pay off as much of your debt as possible, while leaving you with enough property to make a fresh start. Chapter 13 is the most common type of reorganization bankruptcy for consumers—you repay your debts over three to five years. Both kinds of bankruptcy have numerous rules—and exceptions to those rules—about what kinds of debts are covered, who can file, and what property you can and cannot keep.[3] Since companies that are in bankruptcy have all of their debts, including outstanding unclaimed property that they might be holding, administered according to the orders of the federal court system, it would seem that bankruptcy law would trump state unclaimed property law, but this actually depends on whether unclaimed property was already payable or was still in its dormancy period at the time that a holder files for federal bankruptcy protection.

As to property that already passed the period of presumed abandonment and would be deemed reportable as of the date of the bankruptcy filing, states are considered creditors under the Bankruptcy Code, since they have a current right to possession of the abandoned property. Assuming that they make a timely proof of claim, states are entitled to distribution from bankrupt estates to the same extent that the original owner or creditors would have been allowed to collect, had they filed proof of claim in their own right. The practical outcome of this position is that it may permit creditors of bankrupt estates to recover on a portion of the claim (by claiming from the estate under unclaimed property procedures), even though they did not file proof of claim in bankruptcy proceedings.

As to claims against a bankrupt creditor that have not reached the period of presumed abandonment under the unclaimed property law as of the date that the bankruptcy petition was filed, states are not creditors entitled to claim the property, because they have no vested right to title or possession of the property until after the dormancy period has passed. The original true owner would have to file a proof of claim against the bankrupt estate within the federal law's guidelines or the unclaimed property claim is pre-empted by federal law and will not stand in court.[4]

MERGERS AND ACQUISITIONS: SUCCESSOR LIABILITY

When you are in the middle of negotiating a merger with or the acquisition of another company, your target company's unclaimed property may not be in the forefront of your negotiations. This can be a mistake. Without performing the proper due diligence into each company's outstanding unclaimed property liability, you might be purchasing a big headache for which you did not receive proper compensation during your negotiations.

The general consensus is that in a merger transaction, which is essentially a stock acquisition, by operation of law, all assets and liabilities of the merged target company become assets and liabilities of the surviving acquiring company. The merged target company ceases to exist as of the effective date of the merger. The acquiring company becomes the successor to all liabilities of the target by operation of law, including the target's unclaimed property liabilities. The acquiring company becomes the holder with respect to all unclaimed property liabilities of the target. Virtually all state statutes, as well as the 1966, 1981, and 1995 Uniform Unclaimed Property Acts, address this issue and provide for this outcome.[5] As a result, if you are the acquiring company, you had better ensure that you are compensated for the unclaimed property liability of the merged target company.

Another issue might surround how and where to report unclaimed property that you have inherited from a merger. Property that is not yet reportable because it has not yet reached its dormancy date will still be held by the acquiring company until it becomes reportable, according to the laws of priority set out by the U.S. Supreme Court. Property that has the name and address information still attached should be reported to the state of the owner's last known address as it appears on your books and records. Property that does not have names and addresses attached might prove to be more of a challenge. According to the current status of the law in this area, property that has reached the period of presumed abandonment after the successor or acquiring company became the holder should be reported by the successor pursuant to the priority rules of *Texas v. New Jersey*. This means that you should report unknown property to the successor acquiring company's state of incorporation.

Property that the acquiring company becomes the successor in liability to that has already reached its dormancy date and is currently reportable (or past due) is more of a difficult issue. If the property has names and addresses attached, you should definitely report it to the appropriate state unclaimed property office. But what about unknown property or no address property? Should you report it to the merged target company's state of incorporation or to the acquiring company's state of incorporation? The answer is unclear. You should work with your legal counsel and with the state unclaimed property offices of both states to see if one will indemnify the acquiring company against claims of citizens of the other state. While the issue is far from settled, you may get a result that works for you by seeking a settlement with the appropriate states.

ASSET ACQUISITIONS

What about situations where you are just buying the assets of another company, rather than purchasing all of their stock and completing a true merger? How is unclaimed property treated in an asset sale situation? Asset acquisitions are more complicated to analyze. Even if the acquiring company only acquires the assets of the target company, they can still become the new holders of the target's unclaimed property. For example, an acquiring company buys all of the accounts receivable of a target company as one of the assets it acquires. Generally, this will include the accounts of customers with credit balances that have not been offset against any outstanding amounts due to the target company. Some of those credit balances might already be older than the applicable state dormancy period. Other credits will still be within the period of presumed abandonment and will not yet be reportable, but will eventually become reportable unclaimed property for the acquiring company. The acquiring company might also have purchased some unclaimed property liability when it assumed employee payroll accounts, employee benefit plans, and accounts payable that show outstanding checks that have never cleared.

The responsibility for unclaimed property reporting and liability for any potential claims by apparent true owners may depend on the terms of the acquisition agreement. The parties may have specifically or even generally made provisions for such liabilities that can be binding on any unclaimed property audit that either company may become subject to. As discussed earlier, the derivative rights doctrine drives the rights of the state to claim property against a holder. If the terms of the sales contract are considered to be reasonable, the state can only attempt to claim property that could be claimed by the true owner. If the true owner could not successfully collect their unclaimed property from the acquiring company, then the state cannot collect property in an unclaimed property audit.

To prevent any unclaimed property surprises from popping up in a merger or acquisition situation, there are a few questions that you will want to ask:

- What liabilities, credits, uncashed checks, and so forth did the acquiring company become legally responsible for?
- Who is the owner of such property?
- Which entity could the owner of the property sue to collect the amount due?
- Is there any argument that limits the state's rights to step into the owner's shoes (i.e., preemption)?
- Is there any provision that expands the state's rights beyond those the owner itself could exercise (i.e., anti-limitation provisions)?

This is by no means an exhaustive list of all of the legal issues that might crop up during an unclaimed property audit, but they are certainly some of the most common. If you know to ask the right questions up front, you may be able to avoid the pitfalls that these topics can present for you during an audit.

■ NOTES

1. See *Texas v. New Jersey*, 379 U.S. 674 (1965); *Connecticut Mutual Life Ins. Co. v. Moore*, 333 U.S. 541, 68 S.Ct. 682 (1948) *rehearing denied* (1948); *State v. Standard Oil Co.*, 5 N.J. 281, *aff'd* 341 U.S. 428 (1951).
2. 1981 UUPA §29(a) and 1995 UUPA §19(a).
3. "What is Bankruptcy?" http://bankruptcy.findlaw.com/bankruptcy/bankruptcy-basics/bankruptcy-definition.html (accessed on February 3, 2008).
4. See *In re Alan Wood Steel Co.* (Bankr. E.D. Pa 1098); *Arkansas v. Federated Dept Stores, Inc.* (S.D. Ohio 1992); and *In re Drexel Burnham Lambert Groups* (Bankr. S.D. N.Y. 1993).
5. See 1966 UUPA §11(c), 1981 UUPA §17(c), and 1995 UUPA §7(c).

CHAPTER 11

How *Not* to Be a Victim of Unclaimed Property Fraud

You have really reached the home stretch in your unclaimed property project by this point. You have reviewed all of your records, determined your outstanding unclaimed property liability, dutifully disclosed all of your overdue amounts to the appropriate states, and put policies and procedures in place to make sure that your company is fully compliant in the future. You're bulletproof now, right? Not quite . . .

Fraud prevention is the Achilles' heel for every business. Since unclaimed property is held on a company's financial records for such a long period of time, it is a particular target for fraudsters. Abandoned funds can be easily stolen, even by employees of the company itself, when records are not closely monitored and only one or two individuals have oversight of your records. This is not just a matter of loss to your company. Remember, as a holder you are fiscally responsible for all abandoned property in your care until either the true owner returns to claim it or it is properly turned over to the proper state government for safekeeping. If the funds are misappropriated while in your care, you will have to pay *twice:* once to the fraudster, and once to the true owner or the state (whichever contacts you first). If you do not have proper controls in place, you might also be subject to civil action on the part of true owners who lost their property while it was in your care. The states can penalize you for being negligent in caring for unclaimed funds. If you are a publicly held company, you may also face Sarbanes–Oxley repercussions for not having proper financial controls in place. While no business can completely eliminate fraud attempts, they can certainly minimize the impact and stop the most obvious fraudsters from making victims out of them. To prevent fraud, you have to understand how it happens and to recognize the potential perpetrators.

What is fraud? Fraud is defined as "deceit, trickery, sharp practice, or breach of confidence, perpetrated for profit or to gain some unfair or dishonest advantage."[1] Several types of fraud can surround an organization's unclaimed property. One is *misappropriation of assets,* in which a thief steals an entity's assets and manages to adjust the company's financial statements to cover up their theft. This can include embezzling receipts, stealing assets, or causing an entity to pay for goods or services not received. Misappropriation of assets can be accomplished alone or with an accomplice and can be perpetrated by upper management, employees, or third parties. Another fraudulent practice involving unclaimed property is *fraudulent financial reporting,* which is intentional or reckless conduct, whether act or omission, that results in materially misleading financial statements. This can lead to serious Sarbanes-Oxley problems and shareholder unrest. The last fraud practice typically affecting the unclaimed property area is *claims fraud,* which can involve identity theft, false documentation, or money laundering.

PSYCHOLOGY OF FRAUD

Numerous studies have been conducted to analyze just what makes people commit fraud and the circumstances that must exist for them to be successful. Not every fraudster is a career criminal. Apparently, relatively normal law-abiding citizens might commit fraud under certain circumstances. For example, individuals commit fraud to conceal personal expenditures with business assets and to avoid paying taxes. If someone with a relatively low-paying job shows up at the office with a brand-new luxury SUV and explains their newfound wealth away as an inheritance or lottery winnings, you might become suspicious!

There seem to be three elements to the successful commission of fraud: (1) perceived pressure, (2) perceived opportunity, and (3) rationalization. All fraudsters are under some type of *perceived pressure.* This pressure is usually financial pressure, like a high debt load; living beyond their means; a sudden financial reversal in their family, like the loss of a spouse's job; or just plain greed. The fraudster might also be attempting to finance a personal vice like gambling. They might feel that they are underperforming at their jobs financially and that they need to "reorganize" some assets to make their department look more successful. The second element in the commission of fraud is that the fraudster must also recognize a *perceived opportunity* to commit fraud, or in other words, they think they can get away with it. Unclaimed property is at high risk for fraud, because most companies consider it forgotten money, which leads to the perception that it is safe to steal. Often, a lack of controls and individual responsibility surrounding unclaimed property make it an ideal fraud target. Because the escheat accounts can be accessed by many departments, most companies do not have a set of controls to monitor each transaction carefully. The last of the three key elements is *rationalization.* The person or group committing the fraud tries to rationalize their criminal activity by telling themselves that it is not criminal or that they are just borrowing the funds to tide them over the rough times they are currently in. They may believe that they are not hurting anyone, since the money is abandoned anyway, or that they deserve it since they did not get a very good raise recently. Sometimes they think that they have no choice and need to make the company appear more profitable. When all of these elements come together, the fraud is perpetrated with ease and will probably go undetected without some sort of tip to management or an authority that prompts an investigation.

Types of Fraudsters

How a business is organized can lend itself to successful fraud attempts. There are three basic types of fraudsters:

1. The Employee, who defrauds the company for his or her own benefit
2. The Manager, who commits fraud for the benefit of the company
3. The External Fraudster, who commits fraud for the benefit of him- or herself or some third party

Understanding how to identify these types of fraudsters is important to preventing fraud from happening in your organization.

So what does a fraudster look like? They look just like you and me. There is no specific psychological profile for someone that commits fraud. Statistics show that they are usually between the ages of 35 to 44 and are more likely to be male (7 out of 10), they are often older, they are perceived to be more "religious," and they do not really have substance abuse problems. They have usually had significant tenure at their job, with 70% of fraudsters having been with the same organization for more than seven years. The average fraudster sounds like the ideal employee, except for the small fact that they can rob your organization blind!

The employee fraudster is often a long-time employee in a position of trust. He or she often claims not to need any help with the job, does not take many vacations, and appears, on the surface, to be extremely dedicated. These fraudsters are often unveiled when someone becomes suspicious of sudden behavioral changes or wealth that cannot be explained. The fraudster is often living beyond his or her means and may have a gambling or alcohol problem or be conducting an extramarital affair that he or she needs extra cash to support. Employee fraudsters are often hostile to management and are generally unhappy with their pay. They will take unclaimed checks for personal use or will be in collusion with an outside third party to claim uncashed checks.

The management fraudster is often seen by others in the company to be arrogant, egotistical, condescending, and "ethically challenged." He or she is perceived as results-driven, but not worrying too much about how these results are obtained. He or she is hostile to opposition and has different expectations of behavior that is acceptable from employees versus what is acceptable from him- or herself. These fraudsters are often reversing unclaimed credits and checks into income to make the company's bottom line, or at least the results of their departments, seem more profitable.

The external fraudster is usually motivated by greed. The three elements of fraud that apply to most situations do not usually apply to these fraudsters, who are often pathological liars and career criminals. They will commit check fraud, identity theft, and cybercrimes. They can often be part of organized crime rings. These fraudsters have been significantly helped by the identity theft software available on the Internet. There are even books published that tell how to commit identity theft! When these fraudsters are attempting to commit their fraud against your company, they will be loose with facts and have inconsistencies in their background stories. They will appeal to your sense of trust and will be hostile to probing questions. If that does not work, they will often resort to intimidation and will probably make veiled threats of legal action if you do not "return" their unclaimed property.

No matter which of these types of fraudsters has your company's assets in their sights, three factors must be present for them to be successful: the opportunity to commit the fraud, the ability to conceal the fraud, and the ability to avoid punishment. If you take away any of these three factors, you can greatly decrease your exposure to fraudulent activities. If you can eliminate *all* of these factors, it will be almost impossible for someone to commit unclaimed property (or any other kind of fraud) against your company.

Several risk factors can help create a fraud-friendly environment. If your company has very lax internal control over who manages unclaimed property, it will be much easier for someone to alter records and file false claims without creating any suspicion. If there are only one or two individuals in your entire company with any knowledge of how the unclaimed property laws work and how your company manages and tracks unclaimed property, there will be no real ability for any management oversight committee to judge whether the laws are being properly administered and if all of the transactions in that area are legitimate. If you have become aware of fraud within your company and let the culprits go because you did not feel that prosecution was worth your while or because you did not want word to get around that you had been had, then fraudsters are likely to target your company again. Lack of access to information about unclaimed property, ignorance, apathy, incapacity, and a lack of an audit trail are also factors that can increase your company's exposure to unclaimed property fraud.

MITIGATING THE RISK OF UNCLAIMED PROPERTY FRAUD

The most important thing that your company can do to mitigate its unclaimed property fraud risk is to create a good audit trail for all unclaimed property transactions. The audit trail has to begin with proper investigation of any outstanding transactions within a short period of time after they are first initiated and end with either properly returning unclaimed property to the true owners or reporting that unclaimed property in a timely manner to the correct state offices. We have discussed the policy and procedure manual and the internal controls that can help to eliminate unclaimed property fraud, but merely having these procedures will not be enough; the company must follow them to the letter. Management has to exhibit a commitment to these policies and procedures by issuing statements to their employees that the procedures are important and that they expect them to be followed and by giving the parties responsible for performing the unclaimed property compliance the resources they need to complete their work.

The external fraudster is probably going to be the easiest one to stop. While thieves continuously come up with new and better ways to steal identities, you can stop them from victimizing your company by requiring several things from anyone claiming abandoned property from you. Insist on several forms of identification to prove the claimants identity. If the claimant is another business, ask them for their current and/or former Federal Employer Identification Number (FEIN). If the claimant is an individual, ask them for their Social Security number (SSN); verify the year and state of issuance, as well as the validity of the number, and cross-reference it against death records. Require that the claimant tell you the address that they had at the time the property was originally issued in their name (payroll check, utility bill, etc.), and require them to provide their current address as well. Check both of these addresses against your company records. Require proof of death and authority to collect on behalf of a decedent if someone is claiming to be an heir or family of a lost true owner. The decedent's estate will have a claim against you for the unclaimed funds if you pay the money to the wrong person. If the claimant is legitimate, he or she should be able to provide you with most, if not all, of the information that you request. Train your employees to follow these guidelines and, hopefully, you will not be the victim of this type of fraud.

There is nothing more damaging to a company's morale (and financial success) than internal fraud. I had the unfortunate experience of being made aware of a long-time fraud perpetrated against one of my clients by a valued employee, which was not discovered until after the employee's retirement. The employee, a 26-year veteran of my client's accounting team, had systematically bilked the company out of at least $250,000 over a period of years by manipulating vendor files to reissue abandoned checks to a relative who had opened a phony business account at the local bank. While my client chose not to prosecute the employee, who had retired out of state, the effect on the rest of the company's employees was hard to watch. Management became suspicious of employees; employees became suspicious of each other; the once-pleasant work environment deteriorated; and my client had to take a rather large hit to their cash reserves to pay for the unclaimed property assessment that had uncovered the fraud. To help prevent employee unclaimed property fraud, policies and procedures may not be enough. You need to instill a culture of business ethics and fair treatment to keep employees from believing that they can get away with any type of fraud.

The management of an entity cannot act one way and expect others in the entity to behave differently. Research shows that employee theft and wrongdoing occurs less frequently when employees have positive feelings about a company than when they feel abused, threatened, or ignored. Perform background checks on all new employees and make sure that new employees are told when they are hired about your company's policy on wrongdoing. Create a reporting policy that gives every employee the responsibility of reporting suspected corrupt or fraudulent activity to their own supervisors or to another member of management. Make sure that these concerns are properly investigated by an internal audit. You might even establish a hotline where employees could report this behavior anonymously, so that they do not have fear of any type of revenge. You should also consider placing all of your unclaimed funds in a separate holding account or trust account until they are reported. Make it known that your company has a policy of prosecuting thieves and you will make no exception, no matter how small the amount. If you do uncover fraud, make sure that you follow through with your threats of prosecution and advertise the outcome in the office.

Management fraud is a different animal altogether, but it can result in the same audit problems as employee fraud. All you have to do is read the news to see the effect that mishandling unclaimed property and writing it off into income can have on a company. The Banker's Trust case is a perfect example. In 1999, several senior executives, along with Banker's Trust itself, were prosecuted when state auditors found flagrant and widespread abuse of unclaimed property by the bank. Banker's Trust falsified documents and lied about what unclaimed property it had in its possession. With the full knowledge of some of its executives, the bank falsified accounting records and took the unclaimed property into miscellaneous income to make it appear that the escheatable funds were profits instead of liabilities, which is a violation of general state unclaimed property laws. The fine paid by Banker's Trust was more than $50 million and a restatement of their financial statements—Sarbanes-Oxley problems? You bet! If your company is a victim of management fraud, your shareholders will be upset and your financials will be even further affected by the large fine that you will undoubtedly have to pay. The business community is not the only group that has been victimized by management fraud, however. The state of Delaware uncovered a massive employee fraud in late 2007 in which a state employee had colluded with third parties to steal hundreds of thousands of dollars from the state's unclaimed property fund. While this is unfortunate, it just goes to show that unclaimed property is a *huge* temptation for fraudsters.

There is really no way to track just how great the impact of fraud has been on businesses, because fraud is notoriously underreported and often goes unprosecuted. Companies are reluctant to admit that they have been defrauded and, in some cases, the fraud goes undetected. When it is uncovered, it is usually due to tips from someone close to the fraudster, an internal audit, or by accident when looking for something else. To prevent fraud, you have to accept the reality that fraud can happen to your company and then put policies and procedures in place to assess the risk and minimize it as much as possible. Learn how to recognize fraudsters and make sure that your company does not operate in a way that makes you an easy target. Give your employees a safe avenue to report potential fraud and create an ethical business atmosphere. Monitor your unclaimed property accounts closely and look into any irregularities promptly. You know the old saying: "An ounce of prevention is worth a pound of cure." In this case, the money you save will be your own!

NOTE

1. *Dictionary.com Unabridged* (v 1.1), s.v. "fraud," http://dictionary.reference.com/browse/fraud (accessed February 2, 2008). Based on the *Random House Unabridged Dictionary*, Random House, Inc. 2006.

CHAPTER 12

Trends in Unclaimed Property

Now that you know where you are on the map in the unclaimed property universe, you might want to know what attractions you can expect to experience as you continue on your journey. Unclaimed property laws and administrative policies are constantly changing, which makes this area of law both infinitely interesting and continually frustrating. Just when you think that you know everything you need to know, the whole game changes. Some changes that are brewing are easy to spot, however. There are both legal and administrative trends that are either happening right now or that we should not be surprised to see in the near future.

Legislative Trends

While the gray areas of unclaimed property are all too often the only driving force in developing your company's policies and procedures, there are a few states that are endeavoring to provide concrete guidance for holders to follow. State legislatures and administrators are looking to the business community for input and are changing the unclaimed property laws to make them less burdensome administratively for the holder community, while still being protective of owner rights. Here are some of the changes currently being tossed around in the state legislatures.

- *Limitation on expiration dates for gift certificates, gift cards and stored-value cards.* As the past few years have shown, retailers are lobbying hard in their state legislatures to have gift certificates and their progeny removed from the list of escheatable property. In roughly 32 states, retailers have succeeded in having these types of property removed from unclaimed property reporting, but these exemptions are conditional. As consumer groups work harder to protect the rights of gift-card recipients to have a longer amount of time to use their gift cards, we can expect the statutorily mandated minimum useful life span of gift cards to increase. We expect limitations for the expiration of gift cards to require retailers to either (1) prevent the gift cards they issue from expiring at all, or (2) give customers more than two years to use the card without *any* devaluation for dormancy fees or administrative fees to keep gift certificates from becoming reportable unclaimed property.

- *More states with the business-to-business (B2B) exemption.* Unclaimed property holders have been very busy in the past ten years lobbying their legislatures to exempt transactions between businesses from being reportable. There were no states with this exemption 15 years ago. Currently, there are 13 states with this legislation, and we can only expect the number to increase. Texas, for example, has not codified a B2B exemption, but it has adopted an administrative policy that allows holders to skip remitting these types of outstanding transactions. In their unclaimed property report instructions, they inform holders that they do not have to remit transactions that might otherwise be escheatable if the true owner is a current business associate. Let us hope that all of the remaining states jump onto the B2B bandwagon!
- *Move backward to separate report and remit dates.* Back in the dark ages of unclaimed property reporting (i.e., the 1980s), many states required that holders file a preliminary unclaimed property report, do their due diligence, and then turn over the unclaimed property that could not be returned to the rightful owner at a later date. Every state moved away from this bifurcated reporting program, at the insistence of holders, but the old ways might be making a comeback. After the class-action lawsuits against the California Controller, contending that the state's unclaimed property program has been operating in an unconstitutional manner, the current controller, John Chiang, proposed new procedures for holders that report to California. He has bifurcated the reporting process into a preliminary report and final report with payment system that harkens back to the unclaimed property procedures of old. This system is *much* more burdensome for holders; it basically doubles their reporting burden. Let's hope that this flashback to the past is short-lived in California and that none of the other states decide to get nostalgic.

- *Modernization of legislative language to include reloadable cards.* As the manner of currency that consumers use migrates to plastic and away from paper, legislatures are going to be faced with more and more types of reloadable cards, whether they are gift cards, payroll cards, or loyalty program cards with merchandise credits added and subtracted. To collect these types of potentially escheatable property, the states that do not exempt them are going to have to include proper language in their statutes to direct holders to report them. There will also need to be some guidance as to when these cards become dormant, whether it is on the date of the last transaction, the last addition of value to the card, or the last time the balance was checked online. States like Texas are already tackling reloadable gift cards and others are sure to follow.

- *Requirement for electronic reporting.* As budgets allow and as new technology catches up with the state administrators, they are aware how much easier it is to input information that is submitted in an electronic format. Property is added to searchable databases faster and with less transcription error. As more and more states obtain the technology to accept and process electronic unclaimed property reports, more and more of them are going to begin *requiring* holders to file electronically. As it stands, several states require electronic reports from holders with more than a minimum number of line items (usually 25 or more) to report, and we can expect more states to join in. Free unclaimed property reporting software is available from ACS Wagers on the Internet at www.wages.net; it creates electronic reports in the National Association of Unclaimed Property Administrators' (NAUPA's) approved format. Other software providers can also create an electronic reporting solution for your company, but at a significant cost. If your company has not transitioned to a software reporting program as yet, it might be worth looking into, especially if you will be filing in a large number of states. If you are only filing in one or two, the free HRS Pro software offered by ACS Wagers will probably be sufficient for your needs. If you have questions, ask your unclaimed property consultant for a recommendation.

- *Increased aggregate amounts for reporting.* In the past few years, several states have increased their minimum aggregate reporting amounts.

The minimum used to be around $25, but many states have increased their aggregate amount to $50, and it is not uncommon to see a $100 minimum value for unclaimed property to be included in a holder's aggregate amount. The reason for this increased aggregation amount could be varied: business holders are lobbying to get some relief from the burden of performing due diligence on small dollar amounts, and states, generally, will never have to return these small dollar amounts to a true owner since they come with no owner contact information. Whatever the reason, these amounts seem to be creeping steadily higher with no real opposition from holders, businesses or consumer groups.

Non-Legislative Trends

While the laws in each jurisdiction have to be your first source of direction for running your unclaimed property programs, the unwritten policies of each jurisdiction can be very helpful when the law is not clear. Each state unclaimed property administrator has quite a bit of discretion in how he or she conducts his or her programs. Holders who are familiar with these policies can use the information to their advantage in designing unclaimed property programs.

* *Increased audit activity by both state auditors and third-party contract auditors.* With the end of the 1999 NAUPA amnesty initiative, many states have both increased their audit staffs and opened their offices up to bids from multiple outside contractors to perform audits on their behalf. California announced at the 2007 Unclaimed Property Professionals Organization Annual Conference in San Antonio that they had hired more than 15 new auditors in 2006 and that we could all expect a dramatic increase in audit activity. The state of Ohio has hired numerous local accounting firms to conduct audits on companies in their communities on behalf of the state. The biggest contract multistate audit companies are posting record earnings as they audit more and more companies for more and more states each year. There is really no foreseeable end to the amount of money that can be collected through these audits, since only about 20% of U.S. companies are compliant with all of the unclaimed property laws to which they are subject.

- *Advanced technology used by unclaimed property offices.* As new computers and electronic records replace the paper records that used to keep all of the unclaimed property lists, the states are processing unclaimed property reports and claims faster than ever. All of the states have Web sites where you can search for unclaimed property and download instructions for filing unclaimed property reports. Many states are also offering free reporting software. Ohio, for example, even offers one-click negative reports for companies that only have to file a negative or zero report in their state through the Ohio Business Gateway Web site. States are becoming more and more efficient at reuniting true owners with their property. For example, more than 30 states are submitting their unclaimed property records to www.missingmoney.com. Better recordkeeping also means more audits, as states are quite aware of which companies are filing, which are filing only sporadically, and which are not filing at all. You can expect this to lead to more audits. States like California, Wisconsin, Illinois, and Kentucky are even using the World Wide Web to auction off tangible personal property on eBay. While this is controversial, because eBay is considered a bargain-basement auction site where buyers often pay far less than fair market value for the items listed, it is a way for the states to get more eyes and wallets bidding on the items that they previously only auctioned live in local auction houses with a limited number of bidders. The funds from these auctions are put into the unclaimed property fund for the true owners to come back and claim, but money will certainly not replace the actual items and the sentimental value that they may have held.

- *Fewer waivers of penalties and/or interest under audit.* The states have all gone to quite a bit of trouble over the past several years to get the word out to holders and their advisors (accountants, attorneys, etc.) about their obligations to file unclaimed property reports. States are doing everything from sending mass mailings to offering free seminars to alert potential holders that they need to report their escheatable property. For several years, some states offered formal amnesty programs with waivers of penalty and interest for all of the "unknowing" holders to catch up without real punishment (other than handing all of the escheatable property over to the states, that is). Since the states have made such an effort to educate holders about their legal obligations, they are becoming less and less understanding when holders fail to file properly. While most state unclaimed property officials have the discretion to waive penalties and interest for holders that file late, the likelihood that they will just wave you through without a good explanation decreases annually. They are requiring that holders show good faith or good cause for waivers of penalties and interest. Do not be surprised if you are required to give a written explanation that has to be approved before you have penalties waived. Many states will no longer waive interest.

- *Uniform property type codes.* The members of NAUPA have been working very diligently alongside the holder community to develop a much shorter standardized list of property type codes. This project is moving along and should result in an easier filing process once it is put into practice. We can only hope that a uniform holder claim form will not be far behind.

- *Holder Bills of Rights.* The members of the holder community have been quite vocal in voicing their displeasure at the aggressive auditing techniques and overzealous record requests that auditors have used in the past. A few states have implemented administrative procedures, known as Holder Bills of Rights, that attempt to make the process of unclaimed property compliance more standardized and less of an unknown process for holders. In Arizona, for example, there is a new Unclaimed Property Assistance Office to evaluate complaints from holders about such aggressive behavior by Department of Revenue employees. Iowa and Maryland have implemented new appeals procedures for holders who are not satisfied with the results of their unclaimed property audits. These initial efforts are sure to be copied in many more states in the near future. These guidelines should make it easier for holders to manage their relations with the state administrators.

- *No more early reporting.* To ease the burden of administering unclaimed property for holders, many states have traditionally allowed them to report unclaimed property early. The states would allow holders to relieve themselves of the legal responsibility they held to true owners by reporting property before the legal dormancy period had expired under certain circumstances. Usually, the holders did not have a good address for the owners or they had attempted to perform due diligence and their efforts went unanswered. Some holders just wanted to rid themselves of the hassle of administering the property as soon as possible. While some states allowed this in the past, the trend is turning in the other direction. The thought is that true owners are much more likely to seek their property from the holders than from state administrators, especially if the holders would have reported the property to another state than where the property was originally located. Since owners are most likely to find property where they left it, and states are supposed to be doing their best to make sure that owners are reunited with their lost assets, many states are refusing to take property before the law requires that they take it. Even those that will accept property early require written permission from the administrator before the property is reported for a valid transfer of indemnity to take place.

Conclusion

As new and potentially unclaimed property is created every day, there is no real likelihood that the issue is going to go away any time soon. States, under pressure from shrinking budgets and decreasing tax bases, will continue to increase their audit activity to bring money into their coffers that will produce interest to be used for the general good. With increased holder education, interest and penalties will become as common as audit notification letters, and amnesty will be harder and harder to come by. Unclaimed property administrators and holder advocates are working diligently to make the process smoother by standardizing documents and processes where possible. If you are not active in an unclaimed property networking group, look to the Unclaimed Property Professionals Organization or your local bar associations and accounting associations to keep you in the loop about legislative and administrative changes that affect your company and how you report. The time that you invest in keeping current can help you streamline your processes, keep the unclaimed property that you report to a minimum, and keep you out of the audit arena. If you have not yet been contacted for any audit, chances are good that you will be soon. Preparation can make the differences between a few hundred dollars and several thousand dollars owing when your final assessment comes in the mail. As always, if you do not feel that you can tackle your unclaimed property project alone, there are many very talented holders' advocates who can guide you through the process and sophisticated software programs that can ease your compliance burden. Do not be too proud to ask for help; the money you save will be your own!

XYZ Corporation: Unclaimed Property Holder Questionnaire

ORGANIZATION AND HISTORY

Contact Person:
Address:
City: State: Zip:
Phone:
Type of Business:

Total Assets: _____ Revenues: _____
Number of Employees: _____

1. What is the name and title of the officer responsible for compliance with Unclaimed Property laws in your company?

   _____

2. What is the name and title of the person assigned to prepare the annual Unclaimed Property reports in your company?

   _____

3. What is your company's state and date of incorporation?
   a. State: _____
   b. Date of incorporation: _____
4. Has your company ever changed its state of incorporation? YES or NO
   a. If so, when? _____

   _____

5. Are reports filed: consolidated? ‗‗‗‗‗ by division? ‗‗‗‗‗
by subsidiary? ‗‗‗‗‗
   a. List of divisions and subsidiaries:
   b. If your company is a subsidiary or division, list parent:
   c. List any mergers or acquisitions:

6. Are file copies of annual reports of unclaimed property maintained by your company? ‗‗‗‗‗ Are they currently available? ‗‗‗‗‗
   a. If Yes, where are they located? ‗‗‗‗‗‗‗‗‗‗‗‗‗‗
   b. Who has custody? ‗‗‗‗‗‗‗‗‗‗‗‗‗

7. Are reporting procedures or policies relating to unclaimed property documented in procedure or policy manuals for your company? YES or NO
   a. If yes, please provide a copy.
   b. If no, how does your company identify and report unclaimed property?

8. Does your company report unclaimed property to any other states? YES or NO
   a. If yes, please list states and years reports were filed.

9. What source does your company use to determine its reporting responsibilities under the various states' laws?

10. Does your company use the criteria established in *Texas v. New Jersey* when reporting to the states? YES or NO
    a. If no, what are you doing?

11. Does your company report "no address" property to your state of corporate domicile? YES or NO
    a. If no, what is the disposition of such property?

12. Does your company consider any category or type of property exempt from unclaimed property reporting? YES or NO
    a. If yes, please provide details and legal positions.

13. Does your company report the following categories of unclaimed property?
    a. Securities
    b. Mutual fund shares
    c. Dividends
    d. Underlying shares
    e. Funds held for redemption/liquidation
    f. IRA Keogh

g. Fiduciaries

h. Insurance

i. Insurance: Demutualization proceeds

j. Insurance: Proceeds from mature contracts (limiting age contracts)

k. Insurance: Proceeds due beneficiaries

l. Credit memos

m. Vendor checks

n. Wages

o. Dissolution/liquidation

p. Checking

q. Savings

r. Certificates of deposit

s. Official bank checks/money orders

t. Safe-deposit boxes

u. Non-bank money orders

v. Traveler's checks

w. Gift certificates/cards

x. Miscellaneous intangible property

14. Have any policies relating to unclaimed property or service charges thereon been adopted by a formal resolution of the board of directors or a committee?

15. Is your company relying on an opinion from legal counsel regarding its reporting responsibilities under the unclaimed property law of any state?

16. Is your company making any deductions or withholdings from any property that is subject to the unclaimed property reporting?

17. Is it the policy of your company to refund or reinstate any service charges or other amounts deducted if the owner reactivates or claims the property prior to the statutory reporting period?

18. Has your company ever written off stale dated checks or other types of aged credit balances (i.e., accounts receivable credit balances, deposits, withholdings, etc.) to income?

19. If your computer system has changed, list the dates.

20. Provide a list of transaction codes for entries in the general ledger. (For example, adjusting journal entries are usually coded differently than regular cash disbursements.)

Sample Policy and Procedure Manual

XYZ COMPANY
Unclaimed Property Policies and Procedures Manual
Last Updated July 20XX

UNCLAIMED PROPERTY POLICIES AND PROCEDURES

PURPOSE, MAINTENANCE, AND CONTACTS

I. Purpose

[Entity] is dedicated to complying with the unclaimed property reporting laws of every jurisdiction to which it may become accountable. Unclaimed property is generally intangible property that has not been claimed by its true owners for a period of time. It is [Entity]'s goal to limit all payments back to each state by having internal controls in place that will reduce dollars escheated back to each state and return property to the true owner where possible.

Some examples of unclaimed property typically handled by our company include but are not limited to:

- Uncashed payroll checks
- Uncashed vendor checks
- Uncashed member refund checks
- Unused prepaid personal training hours
- Unidentified remittances

II. Information That Must Be Maintained

To properly maintain our unclaimed property records, the following information should be maintained for each outstanding check or credit:

- Name of owner
- Type of property (e.g., payroll check, overpayment, member refund, etc.)
- Identifying numbers, such as check number, vendor number, employee number, and/or member number
- Owner's address (including street address, apartment or suite number, city, state, ZIP code, and country)
- Social Security number and/or Federal Employee ID Number
- Amount due owner before any deductions
- Type of deductions, if any (e.g., service charge, interest)
- Amount of deductions or withholding
- Amount that will be remitted as due
- Interest rate (including percentage rate)

III. Unclaimed Property Contact Person

To ensure that information is disseminated consistently throughout the company and to interested noncompany parties, any inquiry from internal employees or outside parties should be referred to [name(s)], as members of the Unclaimed Property Oversight Committee.

[Name(s)] may be contacted at:

Procedures

I. Filing Requirements

At the end of each quarter, the following items should be delivered to the person involved in unclaimed property filing:

A. List of all checks outstanding that are at least 90 days old
B. List of all checks that were voided during the quarter
C. A detailed reason as to why each check was voided
D. Proper backup, which includes the following for the voided checks:
   1. Copy of voided check
   2. Copy of source document that created liability (invoice, authorization)
   3. Copy of new check if it was to the wrong vendor
   4. Copy of any correspondence
E. List of unidentified remittances that are at least 90 days old; these would be payments that [Entity] has received but does not know where they are from or whose account it is (e.g., membership number, vendor number, invoice number, etc.)
F. List of unidentified credits, accounts receivable credit balances, unidentified credit balances, etc., which would include checks that came to the company with a membership number or vendor number that can easily be identified, but that do not correspond with an invoice on the member or vendor that matches the payment received
G. Copies of bank statements and bank reconciliations for the reporting period (to ensure that outstanding checks and voided checks are correctly noted)

II. Non-Escheatable Property

The following items may not be included in escheatable property if properly documented:

A. Outstanding checks to current employees of the company
B. Outstanding checks for charitable donations
C. Outstanding checks to businesses with which [Entity] has a current business relationship (meaning [Entity] has transacted business with the other business entity within the last 12 to 18 months)

D. Outstanding checks to businesses located in states with a business-to-business (B2B) exemption, which include (as of January 31, 2007):

1. Arizona
2. Florida
3. Illinois
4. Indiana
5. Iowa
6. Maine
7. Maryland
8. Massachusetts
9. North Carolina
10. Ohio
11. Tennessee
12. Virginia
13. Wisconsin

III. Procedure Goals

These procedures will ensure the following:

A. They will reduce the dollar amount escheated to each state.
B. They will enhance the current internal controls of detecting duplicate payment, duplicate invoices being paid, employees receiving additional checks upon termination, and unapplied checks to current members and vendors.
C. They will reduce labor hours spent perpetuating annual unclaimed property reports and reviewing lost dollars for escheatable items.
D. They will reduce any writing off of accounts because they became stale.

IV. Accounts Payable Department Procedures for Outstanding and Voided Checks

At the end of each quarter, the information included in this section must be forwarded to the tax department for each voided check and any check outstanding for 90 days. This information should be completed no later than 30 days after the quarter.

A. Information for the tax department
  1. A copy of each bank reconciliation for the previous three (3) months
  2. Enter each voided or outstanding check on a Microsoft Excel spreadsheet, using the following columns:
     a. Number of owners on check
     b. Type of check (void or outstanding)
     c. Check number
     d. Check date
     e. Void date
     f. Owner's name (last name first)
     g. Social Security number or Federal Employer ID Number, if applicable
     h. Amount of invoice before any deductions
     i. Amount of deductions, if any
     j. Net amount of check
     k. Mailing address (street, apartment/suite)
     l. City
     m. State
     n. ZIP code
     o. Country, if other than United States
     p. Explanation of what happened, if the check is void; if out-standing, is there still an open invoice to be paid with that member/vendor?
     q. Work paper number that will tie to the proper backup required
B. Proper backup for a voided check:
  1. Copy of voided check
  2. Copy of invoice or other source document that created the liability
  3. A detailed description of the reason for the voided check
  4. If duplicate payment, a copy of the new check
  5. If paid to incorrect member/vendor, copy of the new check
  6. If wire sent to member/vendor, copy of the wiring instruction
  7. Any additional pertinent information

C. Proper backup for an outstanding check:
1. Copy of check
2. Copy of invoice or other source document that created the liability
3. A list of any invoices still open to the member/vendor
4. Information about any address changes in the past 90 days
5. Any additional pertinent information

IV. Tax Department Procedures for Unclaimed Property for Outstanding Accounts Payable Checks and Credit Balances

A. Review information from the accounts payable department to verify the following items:
1. Is each item of required information and each column of the spreadsheet complete for each outstanding item?
2. Is the proper backup documentation included?
   a. If not, make a list of the information that is still required and send an email back to accounts payable department
   b. If you have proper information, go to step B.
3. Review the bank reconciliation, and verify that each voided check is on the spreadsheet. If not, make a list of the information for outstanding checks and send an email back to the accounts payable department.
4. Once you have all of the proper information, go to step B.
B. Determine whether the unclaimed property is exempt by using the following exemptions:
1. Is this check to another business with an address in a state with a B2B exemption?
2. Is this check to a charitable organization?
3. Is this check to another business with which [Entity] has a current business relationship?
4. Is this check to a current employee?
   a. If the check is exempt, *note it in the system.*
   b. If the check should be voided, notify the accounts payable department via email and *note it in the system.*
   c. Once you have completed step B, go to step C.

C. Review each line item for credits and determine whether the backup is sufficient, using the following guidelines:

1. Do you have a copy of the check, wiring instructions, or credit memo?

2. Do you have a copy of any correspondence that was received with the check, wire, or credit memo?

3. Do you have a copy of any correspondence from employees in the company regarding this balance?

4. Is the owner of the outstanding amount still a member of [Entity]?

5. If you have sufficient backup, then note this in the system as *not escheatable* and go to step D.

6. Is the company aware of a change in address during the last 90 days? If so, make sure the new address is noted in the system before going to step 7.

7. If you cannot get enough information, then a letter should be sent to the member or vendor asking if they have a prepayment due to them or if they are aware that they are due any amount. The member/vendor should be asked to send this letter back *notarized* with their response to the inquiry. *Note:* This should only happen in rare circumstances, as members/vendors generally do not write checks that are not due to the company.

8. Depending on the response received from the member/vendor, either:

   i. A check will need to be issued, OR

   ii. You can note in the system that the amount is not escheatable If you get no response, list the check/credit as escheatable in the system. Once you have completed step C, go to step D.

D. Now that you have a list of exempt items, escheatable items, and non-escheatable items, extract the escheatable items from the spreadsheet and sort them by state of the owner's last known address. Determine, by state, what the dormancy period for the property is and move items to the unclaimed property holding account, noting the year in which this item of property should be reported to the respective state.

E. *Note:* Before an item is escheated to a state, a due diligence letter will have to go out to the last known address of each true owner 60 to 120 days before the Unclaimed Property Report needs to be filed.

V. Procedures for Payroll Department for Outstanding and Voided Checks

A. At the end of each quarter, the following information must be forwarded to the tax department for each voided check and any check outstanding for 90 days. This information should be completed no later than 30 days after the quarter.

   1. A copy of each bank's reconciliation for the previous three months
   2. Enter each voided or outstanding check on a Microsoft Excel spreadsheet, using the following columns:
      a. Number of owners on checks
      b. Type of check (void or outstanding)
      c. Check number
      d. Check date
      e. Void date
      f. Owner's name (last name first)
      g. Social Security number
      h. Amount of wages before any deductions
      i. Amount of deductions, if any
      j. Net amount of check
      k. Mailing address (street, apartment/suite)
      l. City
      m. State
      n. ZIP code
      o. Country, if other than United States
      p. Is employee currently employed by [Entity]?
      q. Explanation of what happened, if it is a void check; if outstanding, is there still open payroll due to be paid to the employee?
      r. Work paper number that will tie to the proper backup required

B. Proper backup for a voided check includes:

   1. Copy of voided check
   2. Copy of invoice or other source document that created the liability
   3. A detailed description of the reason for the voided check
   4. If duplicate payment, a copy of the new check
   5. If paid to an incorrect employee, a copy of the new check
   6. Date of employee termination (if applicable) and copy of any correspondence concerning last check

7. If wire sent to employee, a copy of wiring instruction

8. Any additional pertinent information

C. Proper backup for an outstanding check:

1. Copy of check

2. A list of any payroll checks still outstanding

3. Whether there has been an address change in last 90 days

4. Whether the paycheck was a bonus or special payment

5. Whether the employee is still on the payroll

6. Whether the employee has been terminated, and if so, the date of termination

7. Any additional pertinent information

VI. Tax Department Procedures for Unclaimed Payroll Checks

A. Review information from the payroll department and verify the following items:

1. Is each column of the spreadsheet completed, and has the proper backup been included? If not, make a list of the information that is still required and send an email back to the payroll department.

2. Review the bank reconciliations and verify that each voided check is on the spreadsheet. If not, make a list of the information that is still needed for voided checks and send an email back to payroll department.

3. Review the bank reconciliations and verify that all outstanding checks over 90 days are listed on the spreadsheet. If not, make a list of the information needed for outstanding checks and send an email back to payroll department.

4. Once you have verified all information present, go to step B.

B. Determine whether the unclaimed property is exempt by using the following:

1. Is the check to a current employee?

2. If the voided check is exempt, note it on the spreadsheet.

3. If the outstanding check should be voided, notify the payroll department via email and note that on the spreadsheet.

4. Once you have completed step B, go to step C.

C. Review each line item for voided checks and determine whether the backup is sufficient using the following guidelines:
1. Do you have a copy of the voided check?
2. Do you have a detailed description of why the check was voided?
3. If it was because of a duplicate payment, do you have a copy of the original check to the employee?
4. If the wrong employee was paid, do you have a copy of the new check to the correct employee?
5. If a wire was sent before the check was cut, do you have a copy of the wiring instructions?
6. If the employee was terminated, do you have any correspondence concerning the last check?
7. If you have sufficient backup, then note this on the spreadsheet as *not escheatable* and go to step D.
8. Has there been a change in address during the last 90 days? If so, make sure that you get the new address before you go to step 9.
9. If you cannot get enough information, then a letter should be sent to the employee asking the employee whether any balance is due; they need to send the letter back with their response, notarized. *Note:* This should only happen in rare circumstances (otherwise the check would have been voided).
10. Depending upon what response you get back from the employee, either:
    a. A check will need to be reissued, OR
    b. You must note on the spreadsheet that the check is *not escheatable*
11. If you get no response, then list the check as *escheatable* on the spreadsheet.
12. Once you have completed step C, go to step D.
D. Review each line item for outstanding checks and determine whether the backup is sufficient using the following guidelines:
1. Do you have a copy of the check?
2. Do you have a list of any paychecks still outstanding?
3. Is the outstanding check a bonus or a special payment?
4. Is the employee still on payroll?
5. If the employee has been terminated, do you have the date of termination?
6. Has there been an address change in the last 90 days?

7. If you feel, from your review, that the check is still valid, write a letter to the employee asking them if they received your check. List out the check date, number, and amount, and include the payroll period that it covered.

8. Depending on the response you receive from the employee, either notify the department that they will need to void the check and reissue, or that they will need to void the check and no balance is due—note this on the spreadsheet as *not escheatable*.

9. If you get no response, go to step E.

E. Now that you have a list of exempt item(s), escheatable items, and nonescheatable items, extract the escheatable items from the spreadsheet and sort them by state. Determine, by state, what the dormancy period is, and make a new column on the spreadsheet noting the year in which the unclaimed property report needs to be filed. *Note:* In most cases, another letter will have to go out to the employees between 60 and 120 days before the unclaimed property report needs to be filed.

Sample Due Diligence Letter

July 29, 2008

James Smith
10110 19th Ave. SE
Apt. #1234
Everett, WA 98208

Dear James,

Upon review of our transaction records, we discovered a discrepancy that temporarily prohibits us from confirming your account balance. Our accounts show an uncashed check in the amount of $70.00 that was issued in May 2004. While this could be a bank error, we require your assistance to resolve this matter.

Please confirm whether your records show a balance due from EndofAll Transactions Corporation that is 120 days or older by checking one of the options and signing below (feel free to provide any supporting documentation). If we receive no response from you, we are required by law to turn the amount over to the Washington Department of Revenue Unclaimed Funds Division by November 1, 2008.

Kindly send your response by *10/13/08*. Please fax this signed and notarized letter to Stacey Reed at (888) 555-1212 or mail to the following address:

EndofAll Transactions Corporation
ATTN: Stacey Reed
2345 Applewood Drive
Ft. Knox, KY 99900

Thank you in advance for your cooperation, and we apologize for any inconvenience.

Sincerely,
Stacey Reed
Corporate Compliance Accountant
EndofAll Transactions Corp.

_____ No amounts are owed to *James Smith* by EndofAll Transactions Corp. that are 120 days or older.

_____ Amounts are owed to *James Smith* by EndofAll Transactions Corp. that are 120 days or older. Please provide a detailed listing and invoice(s) or a description of the reason for the amount if possible.

Signature: _____   Date: _____

Witnessed by me this _____ day of _____, 2008 in the County of _____, in the State of _____, the above mentioned individual signed this document _____.

Notary: _____

State Unclaimed
Property Office Contacts

Alabama
Office of State Treasurer
Unclaimed Property Division
P.O. Box 302520
Montgomery, AL 36130-2520
(888) 844-8400
www.treasury.state.al.us

Alaska
Department of Revenue
Treasury Division
Unclaimed Property Section
P.O. Box 110405
Juneau, AK 99811-0405
(907) 465-3726
www.tax.alaska.gov/programs/programs/index.aspx?23050

Arizona
Department of Revenue
Unclaimed Property Unit
P.O. Box 29026
Phoenix, AZ 85038-9026
(602) 364-0380
www.azunclaimed.gov/

Arkansas

Auditor of State
Unclaimed Property Division
1400 West Third Street, Suite 100
Little Rock, AR 72201-1811
(501) 682-6000
(800) 252-4648
www.arkansas.gov/auditor/unclprop/

California

Office of State Controller
Bureau of Unclaimed Property
P.O. Box 942850
Sacramento, CA 94250-5873
(916) 323-2827
(800) 992-4647 (within CA)
www.sco.ca.gov/col/ucp/index.shtml

Colorado

Office of State Treasurer
Unclaimed Property Division
1120 Lincoln St., Suite 1004
Denver, CO 80203-2136
(303) 894-2443
(800) 825-2111
www.colorado.gov/treasury/gcp/

Connecticut

Office of State Treasurer
Unclaimed Property Division
P.O. Box 5065
Hartford, CT 06102
(800) 833-7318
www.state.ct.us/ott

Delaware

State Escheator
P.O. Box 8931
Wilmington, DE 19899
(302) 577-8220
http://revenue.delaware.gov/information/Escheat.shtml

District of Columbia
Office of the Chief Financial Officer
Office of Finance & Treasury
Unclaimed Property Unit
810 1st St. NE, Room 401
Washington, DC 20002
(202) 442-8181
http://cfo.dc.gov/cfo/site/default.asp

Florida
Department of Financial Services
Unclaimed Property Bureau
P.O. Box 1910
Tallahassee, FL 32302-1910
(850) 410-9253
http://fltreasurehunt.org

Georgia
Department of Revenue
Unclaimed Property Program
4245 International Parkway, Suite A
Hapeville, GA 30354-3918
(404) 968-0490
http://www.etax.dor.ga.gov/ptd/adm/taxguide/ucp.aspx

Hawaii
Department of Budget and Finance
Unclaimed Property Program
P.O. Box 150
Honolulu, HI 96810
(808) 586-1589
www.state.hi.us/budget/uncprop

Idaho
State Tax Commission
Unclaimed Property Unit
P.O. Box 36
Boise, ID 83722-0410
(208) 334-7660
http://tax.idaho.gov/unclaimed.htm

Illinois

Office of State Treasurer
Unclaimed Property Division
P.O. Box 19495
Springfield, IL 62794-9495
(217) 782-6692
www.cashdash.net

Indiana

Attorney General's Office
Unclaimed Property Division
302 West Washington Street, 5th Floor
Indianapolis, IN 46204
(317) 232-6201
www.indianaunclaimed.com

Iowa

Great Iowa Treasure Hunt
Lucas State Office Building
321 E. 12th Street, 1st Floor
Des Moines, IA 50319
(515) 281-5367
www.treasurer.state.ia.us/unclaimed/index.cfm

Kansas

Kansas State Treasurer
Unclaimed Property Division
900 SW Jackson, Suite 201
Topeka, KS 66612-1235
(785) 296-4165
www.kansascash.com/prodweb/up/index.php

Kentucky

Kentucky State Treasury
Unclaimed Property Division
Capitol Annex, Suite 183
Frankfort, KY 40601
(800) 465-4722
www.kytreasury.com/up/u_prop.asp

Louisiana

State Treasurer
Unclaimed Property Division
P.O. Box 91010
Baton Rouge, LA 70821
(225) 219-9400
www.treasury.state.la.us

Maine

State Treasurer's Office
Unclaimed Property Division
39 State House Station
Augusta, ME 04333
(207) 624-7470
www.state.me.us/treasurer/property.htm

Maryland

Comptroller of Maryland
Unclaimed Property Unit
301 West Preston Street
Baltimore, MD 21201-2385
(410) 767-1700
(800) 782-7383
www.marylandtaxes.com/default.asp

Massachusetts

Department of State Treasurer
Abandoned Property Division
1 Ashburton Place, 12th Floor
Boston, MA 02108-1608
(617) 367-0400
www.state.ma.us/treasury/Abp.htm

Michigan

Department of Treasury
Unclaimed Property Division
P.O. Box 30756
Lansing, MI 48909
(517) 636-5320
http://michigan.gov/treasury

Minnesota

Department of Commerce
Unclaimed Property Division
85 7th Place East, Suite 600
St. Paul, MN 55101-3165
(651) 296-2568
(800) 925-5668
www.state.mn.us

Mississippi

State Treasurer
Unclaimed Property Division
P.O. Box 138
Jackson, MS 39205-0138
(601) 359-3600
www.treasury.state.ms.us

Missouri

State Treasurer
Unclaimed Property Division
P.O. Box 1004
Jefferson City, MO 65102
(573) 751-2411
www.treasurer.mo.gov/mainUCP.asp

Montana

Department of Revenue
Attn: Unclaimed Property
P.O. Box 5805
Helena, MT 59604-5805
(406) 444-6900
www.discoveringmontana.com/revenue/programsandservices/
    unclaimedproperty.asp

Nebraska

State Treasurer
State Capitol Building, Room 2003
Lincoln, NE 68509-4788
(402) 471-8497
www.treasurer.state.ne.us/index.asp

Nevada

Office of the State Treasurer
Unclaimed Property
Sawyer Office Building
555 E. Washington Ave., Suite 4200
Las Vegas, NV 89101
(702) 486-4140
http://nevadatreasurer.gov/unclaimed

New Hampshire

State of New Hampshire Treasury
Abandoned Property Division
25 Capitol Street, Room 121
Concord, NH 03301
(603) 271-2619
www.state.nh.us/treasury/Divisions/AP/APindex.htm

New Jersey

Department of the Treasury
P.O. Box 002
Trenton, NJ 08625-002
(609) 292-7500
www.state.nj.us/treasury/taxation/updiscl.htm

New Mexico

Taxation and Revenue Department
Unclaimed Property Office
P.O. Box 25123
Santa Fe, NM 87504-5123
(505) 476-1774
www.state.nm.us/tax

New York

Office of the State Comptroller
Office of Unclaimed Funds
110 State St.
Albany, NY 12236
(518) 270-2200
www.osc.state.ny.us/ouf/index.htm

North Carolina

Department of State Treasurer
Unclaimed Property Program
325 North Salisbury Street
Raleigh, NC 27603-1385
(919) 508-5176
www.treasurer.state.nc.us/dsthome/AdminServices/
    UnclaimedProperty

North Dakota

Unclaimed Property Division
State Land Department
Cash Reunion Program
P.O. Box 5523
Bismarck, ND 58506-5523
(701) 328-2800
www.land.state.nd.us/abp/abphome.htm

Ohio

Department of Commerce
Division of Unclaimed Funds
77 South High Street, 20th Floor
Columbus, OH 43215-6108
(614) 752-5078 (fax)
www.unclaimedfundstreasurehunt.ohio.gov

Oklahoma

State Treasurer
Unclaimed Property Division
4545 North Lincoln Boulevard, Suite 106
Oklahoma City, OK 73105-3413
(405) 521-4273
www.ok.gov/treasurer/

Oregon

Department of State Lands
775 Summer Street, NE, Suite 100
Salem, OR 97301-1279
(503) 378-3805 ext. 450
www.oregon.gov/DSL/UP/index.shtml

Pennsylvania

Treasury Department
Bureau of Unclaimed Property
P.O. Box 1837
Harrisburg, PA 17105-1837
(800) 222-2046
www.patreasury.org/

Rhode Island

Office of the General Treasurer
Unclaimed Property Division
P.O. Box 1435
Providence, RI 02901-1435
(401) 222-6505
www.treasury.ri.gov/unclaimedproperty/

South Carolina

Office of the State Treasurer
Unclaimed Property Program
P.O. Box 11778
Columbia, SC 29211
(803) 737-4771
http://treasurer.sc.gov/

South Dakota

Office of the State Treasurer
Unclaimed Property Division
500 East Capitol Avenue, Suite 212
Pierre, SD 57501-5070
(605) 773-3379
www.sdtreasurer.com

Tennessee

State of Tennessee Treasury Department
Unclaimed Property Division
P.O. Box 198649
Nashville, TN 37219-8649
(615) 741-6499
www.treasury.state.tn.us/unclaim

Texas

Comptroller of Public Accounts
Unclaimed Property Division
Research and Correspondence Section
P.O. Box 12019
Austin, TX 78711-2019
(800) 654-3463
www.window.state.tx.us/up

Utah

State Treasurer
Unclaimed Property Division
341 South Main Street, 5th Floor
Salt Lake City, UT 84111
(801) 320-5360
(888) 217-1203
www.up.utah.gov/

Vermont

Unclaimed Property Office
Office of the State Treasurer
133 State Street
Montpelier, VT 05633-6200
(802) 828-2407
www.vermonttreasurer.gov/

Virginia

Department of the Treasury
Division of Unclaimed Property
P.O. Box 2478
Richmond, VA 23218-2478
(800) 468-1088
www.trs.virginia.gov/ucp/ucp.asp

Washington

Department of Revenue
Unclaimed Property Section
P.O. Box 47477
Olympia, WA 98504-7477

(360) 586-2736
(800) 435-2429
http://dor.wa.gov

West Virginia
Office of State Treasurer
Unclaimed Property Division
P.O. Box 3328
Charleston, WV 25301
(800) 642-8687
www.wvtreasury.com

Wisconsin
Office of the State Treasurer
Unclaimed Property Division
P.O. Box 2114
Madison, WI 53701
(608) 267-7977
www.ost.state.wi.us/home/up.html

Wyoming
State Treasurer's Office
Unclaimed Property
2515 Warren Avenue, Suite 502
Cheyenne, WY 82002
(307) 777-5590
http://treasurer.state.wy.us/uphome.asp

Sample Audit Records Request

CORPOREAL CORPORATION
UNCLAIMED PROPERTY REVIEW

The following documents may be needed in preparation for the unclaimed property review. Please be advised that this list is inclusive, and certain categories of documents may not be applicable to your company's unclaimed property issues.

I. General Information

- _____ A. Internal audit reports
- _____ B. Chart of accounts
- _____ C. Policies, procedures, and practices detailing the flow of accounts including payroll, accounts receivable, accounts payable, and any other areas containing disbursements accounts or credit balances
- _____ D. Policies, procedures, and practices detailing the voiding of checks and the taking of such into miscellaneous income
- _____ E. Organizational chart for YOUR COMPANY and subsidiaries
- _____ F. Any existing unclaimed property procedures for YOUR COMPANY
- _____ G. Unclaimed property reports filed for YOUR COMPANY
- _____ H. General ledger trial balances for 1991–present

_____ I.   Financial statements for 1991–present

_____ J.   List of bank accounts opened and closed from 1991–present

_____ K.   List of active bank accounts

II. Payroll

_____ A.   Outstanding check register for payroll 1991–present

_____ B.   Any journal entries taking voided payroll checks into miscellaneous income

_____ C.   Void check register for payroll for 1991–present

III. Accounts Payable

_____ A.   Outstanding checklist for accounts payable 1991–present

_____ B.   Any journal entries taking voided accounts payable checks into miscellaneous income

_____ C.   Void check register for accounts payable 1991–present

IV. Accounts Receivable

_____ A.   Listing of outstanding aged credit balances

_____ B.   Any journal entries taking outstanding credit balances into miscellaneous income

_____ C.   Any journal entries taking unidentified or unapplied payments into miscellaneous income

V. Bank Accounts

_____ A.   Bank reconciliations for 1991–present (payroll, accounts payable, and royalties).

_____ B.   A list of active and closed bank accounts, including open and closed dates, during look-back period (disbursement accounts).

VI. Royalties

_____ A.   Outstanding checklist for royalties 1991–present

_____ B.   Any journal entries taking voided royalty checks into miscellaneous income

_____ C.   Void check register for royalties 1991–present

Summary of Current Gift Certificate Law

Alabama

Escheat   In general, gift certificates are presumed abandoned three years after being sold; however, gift certificates issued by retailers are exempt from this provision. *Alabama Code § 35-12-72(a)(17); §35-12-73(b)(1)*

Alaska

Escheat   Gift certificates are presumed abandoned after being unclaimed by owner for three years. The amount abandoned is equal to the full price paid by the purchaser. *Alaska Statute § 34.45.240*

Arkansas

Arkansas has enacted the Fair Gift Card Act *(¶ 30,412)*, which prohibits issuance of gift certificates or cards subject to expiration or fees less than two years from issuance. Prominent disclosures of expiration and fee provisions are required. *Laws of 2007, Act 304, approved March 16, 2007, effective 90 days after adjournment*

Escheat   Gift certificates are not considered property and therefore are not subject to escheat laws. *Arkansas Statutes Annotated § 18-28-201(13)(B)*

Expiration   There can be no expiration earlier than two years from the date of issuance; the expiration date must be disclosed in a conspicuous manner. *Arkansas Statutes Annotated § 44-88-703(a) and (c)*

Fees   Fees may be charged beginning two years from the date of issuance; notice must be conspicuous. *Arkansas Statutes Annotated § 44-88-703 (c)*

California

Expiration   Gift certificates cannot contain expiration dates. *California Code § 1749.5(a)(1)*
   A gift certificate sold without an expiration date is valid until redeemed or replaced. *California Code § 1749.5(c)*
   Gift cards cannot contain a service fee until the gift card has been inactive for two years, the remaining value is not more than $5, and the service fee is not more than $1 per month. *California Code § 1749.5(a)(2), 1749.5(e)*

Redemption   Any gift certificate sold after January 1, 1997 is redeemable in cash for its cash value, or subject to replacement with a new gift certificate at no cost to the purchaser or holder. *California Code § 1749.5(b)*

Disclosure   Gift certificates handed out by the issuer to the consumer pursuant to an awards, loyalty, or promotional program, as well as gift certificates sold below face value or those issued for a food product are permitted to contain an expiration date, as long as the date appears in at least ten-point font on the front of the gift certificate. *California Code § 1749.5(d)*

Gift Cards   Gift cards are covered under the definition of "gift certificates," except when a gift card is usable with multiple sellers of goods. *California Code § 1749.45(a)*

Colorado

Escheat   Gift certificates that can be redeemed for cash are subject to escheat if unclaimed for five years; certificates redeemable for goods or services are not subject to escheat. *Colorado Revised Statutes § 38-13-108.4*

Connecticut

Expiration   Gift certificates sold after August 16, 2003 cannot contain expiration dates. Gift certificate sellers are required to obtain the address of the owner and maintain a record of such address. *Connecticut Public Act No. 03-1, Section 84*

Redemption Unclaimed gift certificates are considered abandoned three years after the gift certificate was either purchased or last used. *Connecticut Public Act No. 03-1, Section 74*

However, this does not prevent the holder from honoring a gift certificate, as reimbursement can be sought from the Treasurer. *Connecticut Public Act No. 03-1, Section 84*

Disclosure As of August 16, 2003, gift certificates cannot contain expiration dates.

Gift Cards Gift cards are covered under the definition of "gift certificates." *Connecticut Public Act No. 03-1, Section 66(5).*

Delaware

Escheat In the event that an owner dies intestate, is missing for more than five years, or abandons the certificate, a gift certificate reverts to the state. *Delaware Code Annotated tit. 12 § 1197 et seq.*

District of Columbia

Escheat Certificates unclaimed for five years are presumed abandoned. *D.C. Code Annotated § 41-101 et seq.*

Florida

Florida has enacted a new law *(¶30,912)* prohibiting expiration dates, post sale charges, and fees for gift certificates and stored value cards. *Laws of 2007, Chapter 256, approved and effective June 28, 2007*

Georgia

Disclosure Any expiration date or dormancy/nonuse fee must be conspicuously printed. *Georgia Code § 10-1-393(b)(33)(A)(ii)*

Escheat Certificates unclaimed for five years are presumed abandoned. *Georgia Code § 44-12-205*

Hawaii

Expiration and Fees   Effective July 1, 2005, gift cards may not expire within two years of issue, and no fees may be charged for their use. *Consumer's Union*

Idaho

Escheat   Certificates without expiration dates unclaimed for five years are presumed abandoned. *Idaho Code § 14-514*

Certificates with expiration dates displayed do not constitute abandoned property. *Idaho Code § 14-502(2)(b)*

Illinois

Expiration and Fees   Effective January 1, 2005, gift cards may not have an expiration date or service fees, or they risk escheat to the state. *Consumer's Union*

Indiana

Escheat   Gift certificates are exempt from unclaimed property laws. *Indiana Code § 32-34-1-1*

Iowa

Expiration   Iowa allows sellers of gift certificates to have expiration dates.

Fees   No fees may be charged without a contract. *Iowa Code § 556.9*

Redemption   An issuer of a gift certificate shall not deduct from the face value of the gift certificate any charge imposed due to the failure of the owner of the gift certificates to present the gift certificate in a timely manner, unless a valid and enforceable written contract exists between the issuer and the owner of the gift certificate pursuant to which the issuer regularly imposes such charges and does not regularly reverse or otherwise cancel them. *Iowa Code § 556.9(2)*

Gift Cards   Gift cards are covered under the definition of "gift certificate." *Iowa Code § 556.9(2)*

Kansas

Expiration Effective January 1, 2007, gift certificates with expiration dates must expire no less than five years after the date of purchase. Cards without expiration dates are valid until redeemed or replaced. *2006 H.B. 2658*

Fees No fees may be charged during the first 12 months following issuance. *2006 H.B. 2658*

Kentucky

Expiration Gift certificates with expiration dates must expire no less than one year after the date of purchase. Cards without expiration dates printed on the front or back are valid until redeemed or replaced. *Kentucky Rev. Stat. § 367.890*

Fees No fees may be charged prior to expiration. *Kentucky Rev. Stat. § 367.890(3)*

Louisiana

Expiration An expiration date cannot be less than five years from the date of issuance. It is unlawful for a person to sell a gift certificate with a service fee or dormancy fee, though the seller can impose a one-time handling fee that shall not exceed one dollar per gift certificate. *Louisiana Revised Statute § 1423(B)*

A gift certificate sold without an expiration date shall be valid until redeemed or replaced. *Louisiana Revised Statute § 1423*

Fees In general, no service fees, although a one-time handling fee of $1 or less is permissible. *Louisiana Revised Statute § 1423(B)(2)*

Disclosure Expiration dates shall appear in capital letters in at least ten-point font on the gift certificate. *Louisiana Revised Statute §1423(B)*

Gift Cards Gift cards are covered under the definition of "gift certificate." *Louisiana Revised Statute §1423(A)*

Note: The provisions of §1423 do not apply to gift certificates distributed to a consumer pursuant to an awards loyalty or promotional program without anything being given in exchange for the gift certificate by the consumer. The provisions also do not apply to gift certificates sold below face value or donated to nonprofits, or to gift certificates that are usable with multiple sellers of goods. *Louisiana Revised Statute §1423(D)*

Maine

Expiration   A period of limitation may not be imposed on the owner's right to redeem the gift obligation. *Maine Revised Statutes 33 § 1953(G)*

Redemption   A gift obligation is considered abandoned three years after December 31 of the year in which the gift obligation occurred. A period of limitation may not be imposed on the owner's right to redeem the gift obligation. The amount unclaimed is the face value of the gift obligation, except that the amount unclaimed is 60% of the gift obligation's face value if the issuer of the gift obligation does not impose a dormancy charge. Fees or charges may not be imposed on gift obligations unless they are noted on the gift obligation and are in accordance with section 1956. The amount of these charges or fees may not be unconscionable. *Maine Revised Statutes 33 § 1953(G)*

Disclosure   Fees or charges may not be imposed on gift obligations unless they are noted on the gift obligation and are in accordance with section 1956. *Maine Revised Statutes 33 § 1953(G)*

Gift Cards   Gift certificates and gift cards are both covered under the definition of "gift obligation." *Maine Revised Statutes 33 § 1952*

Maryland

Expiration   Gift certificates must be valid for not less than four years. Any expiration date must be clearly disclosed. *Maryland Commercial Code Ann. § 14-1319; 14-1320*

Fees   Fees must be disclosed, and no fees may be charged within four years of purchase. *Maryland Commercial Code Ann. § 14-1319; 14-1320*

Escheat   Gift cards are exempt from the unclaimed property act. *Maryland Commercial Code Ann. § 17-101(m)*

Massachusetts

Expiration   A gift certificate sold or offered to be sold shall be valid for not less than seven years after its date of issuance. *Massachusetts General Laws 200A §5D*

A gift certificate without an expiration date will not expire. *Massachusetts General Laws 200A § 5D*

Redemption   Notwithstanding any general or special law to the contrary, upon a gift certificate being redeemed for at least 90% of its face value, a consumer shall make an election to receive the balance in cash or to continue with the gift certificate. *Massachusetts General Laws 200A § 5D*

Since the gift card must be redeemable in full value for seven years, issuers are not allowed to deduct service charges or dormancy fees. As of April 1, 2003, issuers of gift certificates that have expired may retain the unredeemed amount on a gift certificate. *Massachusetts General Laws 200A § 5D*

Disclosure   The date of issuance and the expiration date shall be clearly identified on the face of the gift certificate or gift card, with a banked dollar value clearly printed upon a sales receipt transferred to the purchaser or holder of the electronic card through means of an Internet site or a toll-free information telephone line. *Massachusetts General Laws 200A §5D*

Gift Cards   Gift cards are covered under the definition of "gift certificate." *Massachusetts General Laws 255D §1*

Michigan

Escheat   Gift certificates unclaimed for more than five years are deemed abandoned in the amount of the purchase price. *Michigan Comp. Laws § 567.235*

Minnesota

Escheat   Gift cards are exempt from the definition of intangible property. *Minnesota Stat. § 345.39*

A new Minnesota law *(¶32,314)* prohibits expiration dates and service fees for gift certificates and gift cards. *Laws of 2007, Chapter 93, approved May 21, 2007, effective August 1, 2007*

Mississippi

Escheat   Gift certificates unclaimed for more than five years are deemed abandoned. *Mississippi Code Ann. § 89-12-14*

Missouri

Escheat   Gift certificates redeemable only for merchandise are reportable at 60% face value. The owner shall be reimbursed at full value. *Missouri Rev. Stat. § 447.500 et seq.*

Montana

Expiration and Fees   Gift certificates may not expire, and no fees may be charged. *Montana Code Ann. § 30-14-108*

Nebraska

Disclosure   Expiration dates and all types of fees must be clearly disclosed on the gift card or certificate. *Nebraska Rev. Stat. § 69-1305.03*

Nevada

Expiration   An expiration date or a toll-free number to call to enquire about expiration must be printed on the certificate. *Nevada Rev. Stat. § 598.0921(1)(a)*

Fees   Fees must be disclosed and may not exceed $1/month and may not be imposed within 12 months of issuance. *Nevada Rev. Stat. § 598.0921(1)(b)*
   Effective October 1, 2007, issuers are prohibited from charging a service fee for inactivity of less than three continuous years. *2007, Chapter 363*

Gift Cards   Gift cards are covered under the definition of "gift certificate." *Nevada Rev. Stat. § 598.0921(3)(a)*

New Hampshire

Expiration   No expiration for certificates valued at less than $100. Certificates worth in excess of $100 expire when escheated to the state as abandoned property. *New Hampshire Rev. Stat. Ann. § 358-A:2*

Fees   Service fees are prohibited. *New Hampshire Rev. Stat. Ann. § 358-A:2*

New Jersey

Expiration   Expiration must not occur less than 24 months from the date of sale. Any expiration date must be disclosed as specified. *New Jersey Rev. Stat. § 56:8-110(a)(1)*

Fees   No dormancy fee within 24 months of issuance or within 24 months of the most recent activity. Fees may not exceed $2/month and must be disclosed as specified. *New Jersey Rev. Stat. § 56:8-110(a)*

New Mexico

Escheat   Gift certificates are presumed abandoned three years after December 31 of the year sold. If redeemable for merchandise only, the amount abandoned is 60% of the certificate's face value. *New Mexico Stat. Ann. § 7-8A-1 et seq.*

Expiration   No expiration is allowed earlier than 60 months from the date of issuance. If an expiration date is not conspicuously stated on the certificate, then it is assumed to have no expiration date, and is valid until redeemed or replaced. *2007 Chapter 125*

Fees   No fees of any kind may be charged. *2007 Chapter 125*

New York

Expiration   The expiration date must be disclosed. *Laws of New York § 396-i(3)*

Fees   Any fees must be disclosed; fees may not be assessed before the thirteenth month following issuance. *Laws of New York § 396-i*

Redemption   No monthly service fees may be assessed against the balance of a gift certificate prior to the thirteenth month of dormancy. *Law of New York § 396-i(5)(b)*

Disclosure   New York state law (*Laws of New York §396-i(3)*) states:

The terms and conditions of a gift certificate shall be disclosed to the purchaser:

(a)(i) on a sign conspicuously posted stating "TERMS AND CONDITIONS ARE APPLIED TO GIFT CERTIFICATES/GIFT CARDS"; or (ii) conspicuously stated in an offer made by mail thus: "TERMS AND CONDITIONS ARE APPLIED TO GIFT CERTIFICATES/GIFT CARDS"

(b) For purchases via electronic, computer, or telephonic means, the statement "TERMS AND CONDITIONS ARE APPLIED TO GIFT CERTIFICATES/GIFT CARDS" shall be stated prior to the customer's purchase of the gift certificate or conspicuously written within the electronic message offering a gift certificate for purchase.

I. All advertisements or promotions for gift certificates shall include a notice in like or similar term to the following:

"TERMS AND CONDITIONS ARE APPLIED TO GIFT CERTIFICATES/GIFT CARDS." *Laws of New York § 396-i(2-a)* The terms and conditions of a gift certificate store credit shall be clearly and conspicuously stated thereon. Terms and conditions shall include the expiration date, whether any fees are assessed against the balance of the gift certificate, and whether a fee will be charged for the replacement of a gift certificate that is lost, stolen, or destroyed. Additional terms and conditions including, but not be limited to, policies related to refunds, warranties, changes in terms and conditions, assignment and waiver shall be conspicuously printed: (a) on the gift certificate; or (b) on an envelope or packaging containing the gift certificate, provided that a toll free telephone number to access the additional terms and conditions is printed on the gift certificate; or (c) on an accompanying printed document, provided that a toll free telephone number to access the additional terms and conditions is printed on the gift certificate.

Gift Cards   Gift cards are covered under the definition of "gift certificate." *Laws of New York § 396-i(1)*

North Carolina

Escheat   A gift certificate bearing an expiration date is deemed abandoned after three years of dormancy. *North Carolina Gen. Stat. § 116B-53(c)(8)*

Gift certificates are not deemed abandoned if they state that they do not expire, bear no expiration date, or state that their expiration date does not apply in North Carolina. *North Carolina Gen. Stat. § 116B-5354(b)*

Fees Effective December 1, 2007, disclosure of any maintenance fees charged for gifts certificates is required, and no fee may be charged within one year of purchase. *§ 66-67.5*

North Dakota

Expiration and Fees Expiration dates must be not less than six years from issuance. Service fees are prohibited. *North Dakota Cent. Code § 51-29-02*

Ohio

Expiration and Fees Expiration dates must be not less than two years from issuance. Service fees may not be charged within two years of issuance. *Ohio Rev. Code Ann. § 1349.61*

Oklahoma

Expiration Expiration dates must be at least 60 months from the date of purchase. Certificates with no expiration date are valid until redeemed or replaced. *Oklahoma Stat. tit. 15 § 797*

Fees Prohibited unless the certificate has a value of $5 or less, the fee is $1/month or less, and the card has not been active for at least 24 months. *Oklahoma Stat. tit. 15 § 797*

Oregon

Expiration Effective January 1, 2008, the sale of a gift card that has an expiration date is prohibited unless the expiration date is disclosed, the card is sold at a cost below face value, and the card does not expire until at least 30 days after sale. *2007, Chapter 772*

Pennsylvania

Escheat Gift certificates are deemed abandoned if unredeemed for two or more years after expiration or five years from issuance if no expiration is specified. Certificates without any fees or expiration date are exempt from these provisions. *Pennsylvania Cons. Stat. tit. 72, § 1301 et seq.*

Rhode Island

Expiration   It shall be unlawful for any person, firm, or corporation of any kind to charge additional monthly or annual service or maintenance fees on gift certificates or to limit the time for the redemption of a gift certificate or to place an expiration date upon the gift certificates. *General Laws of Rhode Island 6-13-12*

No gift certificate or any agreement with respect to such gift certificate may contain language suggesting that an expiration date may apply to the gift certificate. *General Laws of Rhode Island 6-13-12*

Redemption   A gift certificate issued by a business association that remains unredeemed for more than three years after issuance is presumed abandoned. *General Laws of Rhode Island 33-21.1-14(a)*

In the case of a gift certificate, the amount presumed abandoned is the face amount of the certificate itself. *General Laws of Rhode Island 33-21.1-14(b)*

Gift Cards   Gift cards are covered under the definition of "gift certificate." *General Laws of Rhode Island 6-13-12*

South Carolina

Expiration   There shall be no expiration less than one year from the date of purchase unless disclosed as specified. *South Carolina Code Ann. § 39-1-55(B)*

Fees   Fees are prohibited unless disclosed as specified. *South Carolina Code Ann. § 39-1-55(C)*

South Dakota

Escheat   A gift certificate that is unclaimed by its owner for more than five years after becoming payable is deemed abandoned. *South Dakota Cod. Laws Ann. § 43-41B-15*

Tennessee

Expiration   There shall be no expiration within two years of issuance; the gift card is valid until redeemed or replaced if sold without a valid expiration date. *Tennessee Code Ann. § 47-18-127*

Fees   Issuance fees are prohibited; no service fees are allowed within two years of issuance. *Tennessee Code Ann. § 47-18-127*

Texas

Expiration   The expiration date must be disclosed as specified. *Texas Bus. & Com. Code Ann. § 35.42*

Fees   Handling, access, and replacement fees may be charged. Reasonable dormancy fees may be assessed after the first anniversary of the initial sale. All fees must be disclosed as specified. *Texas Bus. & Com. Code Ann. § 35.42*

Utah

Escheat   A gift certificate valued at more than $25 and unclaimed for 5 years is deemed abandoned. *Utah Code Ann. § 67-4a-211*
    The Utah Consumer Sales Practices Act *(¶34,410)* has been amended to make it a deceptive practice to issue a gift certificate with undisclosed expiration date or fee deduction provisions.

Vermont

Expiration
Gift certificates shall be valid for not less than three years from the date of issuance. Certificates without a clearly marked or available expiration date are deemed to have no expiration date. *Vermont Stat. Ann. tit. 8, § 2702*

Fees   Fees and service charges are prohibited. *Vermont Stat. Ann. tit. 8, § 2703.*

Virginia

Expiration   Any gift certificate with an expiration date must include a statement containing the expiration date or a telephone number or Internet address where the owner can obtain information regarding expiration. *Virginia Code § 59.1-531*

Fees   Any gift certificate that loses value over time must include a telephone number or Internet address where the owner can obtain information regarding this loss of value. *Virginia Code § 59.1-531*

Glossary

Abandoned (Unclaimed) Property   Tangible or intangible property that has gone unclaimed by its rightful owner.

Activity   Action taken on property *by the owner,* which may include making a deposit, a withdrawal, a written memorandum to the holder, or any action that state statutes deem adequate.

Aggregate   The threshold dollar value of an individual owner's account that will require owner detail and due diligence efforts. (For example, if the aggregate is $25, all individual outstanding unclaimed property items equal to or greater than $25 must be identified on the report, and due diligence efforts must be performed to attempt to locate the true owner of the items before they can be reported to the appropriate state agency.)

Custodian   An individual or entity that holds property until it is delivered to the rightful owner. Most states' laws make the unclaimed property division a custodian of the property remitted to the state.

Due Diligence   The degree of effort required by law that a holder must perform to find the rightful owner of an item of unclaimed property before remitting the property to the state.

Dormancy Period   The period of time that transpires after the date when an owner generated any action on his or her property.

Dormancy Date/Date of Last Activity   The date of last contact by the owner, as evidenced in the records of the holder.

Escheat   A transfer of property that makes the state the legal owner of the transferred property. Few states operate under an escheat law as it relates to unclaimed property.

Holder   The entity that is in possession of, or controls, abandoned or unclaimed property until it is transferred to the state on behalf of the lost owner.

Indemnification   An agreement that protects a party from loss by transferring the responsibilities to a third party.

Intangible Personal Property   Property that is represented by a symbol. Stock certificates and savings bonds represent ownership interest in a company. A savings bond represents an obligation to pay the face value.

Rightful Owner   A person or entity who has the legal right to unclaimed or abandoned property.

Index